MW00851617

Ohio Ghost Stories and Spooky Legends—The Classics

ISBN-13: 978-1-940087-44-3

21 Crows Dusk to Dawn Publishing, 21 Crows, LLC

Yes, I went to these places. I have been to over 1500—and still counting. I just do not believe a storyteller can get a true feel for a story, legend, or folklore and tell it properly and with the respect it deserves without taking in the area and people from where the story comes.

The stories and legends in this book are for enjoyment purposes and taken from many different resources. Many have been passed down and have been altered along the way. I attempt to sort through the many different variations found on a story and find the most popular and the most supported by historical evidence/ verbal interviews. Not all sources and legends can be substantiated. Public properties may become private after the printing of the book or they may simply be listed with the address so you know the historical area where the story originated. Listing the GPS and address does not mean you can visit. Regardless if the area is listed as private or not, please respect the landowner and do not disturb their privacy, nor trespass. Readers assume full responsibility for use of information in this book. Please use common sense

Southwestern Ohio

Southeastern Ohio

Northwestern Ohio

Northeastern Ohio

Central Ohio

Citations

Southwestern Ohio

Hamilton County

Richardson Forest Preserve
4000 W Kemper Road
Cincinnati, Ohio 45251
39.309911, -84.608988

Lick Road—The Legend of Amy

Lick Road ends at Richardson Forest Preserve. When visiting, make sure you follow park rules—it closes at dusk. It is creepy even in the daylight with dead deer carcasses littering the roadway leftover from hunters using the preserve.

Lick Road winds its way through farmland, then makes a dead-end at Hamilton County Park District's Richardson Forest Preserve. A mysterious legend surrounds this isolated cul-de-sac and the path along Banklick Creek, leading to a bridge. It centers around a girl named Amy, murdered by her boyfriend then dumped into the creek. Her ghostly form winds its way down the path. If you park at the end of the road and honk three times, she appears. If you sit in your car, condensation will form on the windshield with the words HELP ME written in the misty film.

Brown County

Old Lafferty Road and Chicken Hollow Road
Lafferty Road/Chicken Hollow Road
Ripley, Ohio 45167
38.774345,-83.773953

Calico Lady

Where Lafferty Road meets Chicken Hollow Road and a dead woman haunts those who pass.

Old Lafferty Road in Brown County near Ripley is impassable for cars now. It runs along a creek called Lafferty Run and is a rugged dirt trail with signs of its past still viewable in the old rock fence rows and stone foundations. Years earlier, it was the remote and spooky place thrill-seekers would travel along to find the Calico Lady. If you called out her name three times, the ghostly figure of an old lady would appear dressed in calico clothing and carrying a bucket in her three-fingered hand while cats scattered with yowls at her feet. But, you may still be able to find her. She sits on a guardrail at Lafferty and Chicken Hollow roads and screams curses at passersby.

Clermont County

Lucy Run Cemetery Road and Lucy Run Cemetery

3755 Lucy Run Cemetery Road
Batavia, Ohio 45103
39.04280, -84.19250

Lucy Run

Lucy Run Cemetery (right) and Lucy Run, the creek, (left). A ghostly young woman relives her last moments and searches for her grave.

In the early 1800s, the Charles Robinson family built a homestead along a stream near Amelia in Clermont County. Over time, the family and close neighbors were buried at a small cemetery on Robinson's plot of land at the base of a small hill separated from the creek by a worn dirt road. Sometime throughout the years, a young woman living near the Robinsons named Lucy was going to be wed to a strapping young man popular in the community.

But only days before the marriage, he awakened the family with a hard knock upon Lucy's father's door at midnight and during a thunderstorm. The father and daughter rushed to answer the banging of fist to wood in their nightclothes. When the door burst open, and the father held a lantern aloft, the face of the young woman's fiancé was exposed in the pale light. He declared hastily he had found another to love. He would no longer marry her.

Quickly, he left while the heartbroken Lucy sobbed into her hands. Then, in a miserable fit of anger and without bothering to change into day attire, the spurned woman grabbed up her young horse and chased him down the mud-slick road beside the flooded creek through the stormy night. Suddenly, a crack of thunder exploded into the night sky, and the horse bucked, frightened. The stunned girl was violently thrown into the surging waters. She drowned in the torrent bursting past the shoreline and disappeared into its depths.

Since then, her ghostly form glides up from the creek named for her, Lucy Run. She limps across the road in her pale white nightgown from the place she perished to the cemetery bearing her name, Lucy Run Cemetery. She searches for a grave she will never find because the creek never gave up her lifeless body, and no headstone was placed there to mark her passing.

Clermont County

Utopia
3833 Main Street (US-52)
Georgetown, Ohio 45121
Church: 38.776009,-84.056359
Marker: 38.77621,-84.056518

Dying to Get Into Utopia

Utopia today. Where ghosts rise from their watery grave.

The little river town was among a few dozen experimental societies founded by Frenchman Charles Fourier in the 1830s and 1840s. He wanted to build a perfect utopian society based on the equal sharing of money and labor by those within the community, hence the name: Utopia. In return for a small house and land, families would pay $25.00 per year and work together as one and hopefully avoid the turmoil and depressed economy that had tainted their society in earlier years.

Fourier followers built private residences and a communal brick house, but the commune failed miserably. Within a couple of years, the community was abandoned and sold to John Wattles, the leader of a spiritualist group. Their philosophies blended traditional Christian beliefs along with communicating with the dead. The closeness to the Ohio River caught Wattles's eye—running water was also of spiritual significance to the religion.

The moving waters were so crucial that in 1847 and against warnings of a flood, members moved a two-story brick building right up to the bank of the Ohio River. Only partially finished, 32 people gathered for a party on the rainy eve of December 13th, 1847. As a dance pursued, the Ohio River flooded its banks, surrounding the building and causing the walls to collapse. Seventeen of the followers were drowned or swept into the frigid floodwaters and succumbed to hypothermia. John Wattles and his wife were among those present but escaped before the collapse. Those dead rise here in the Ohio River, and their ghosts waver where they drowned along the flooded shore. Some see them as mists, others as dancing lights and apparitions dripping on the banks.

Remnants of old Utopia still remain.

Adams County

Cherry Fork Cemetery
14348 OH-136
Winchester, Ohio 45697
38.87959, -83.61529

A Grave Yawns

Cherry Fork Cemetery where balls of light flitting from an unmarked grave have frightened people for years.

On Tuesday, December 19th of 1893, 80-year-old Luther "Pitt" Rhine and his 71-year-old wife, Martha, were found on their small farm with their skulls crushed and their throats slashed from ear to ear in their little farmhouse along a stream called Elk Fork, not far from West Union. They had been sleeping when attacked.

Sixteen-year-old Roscoe Parker, a boy of dubious character, who did odd jobs for the couple, had helped Luther drive a calf to nearby Winchester for butchering the day before. When questioned, law enforcement found Roscoe's bloodied clothing and a pair of Luther's stockings hidden in his bed along with five dollars of the Rhine's money identified as being paid for the calf. The boy was arrested but never made it to court. Instead, an angry mob whisked Roscoe off in his underclothes, hanged him, and riddled his body with bullets.

They buried Roscoe Parker's body in the pauper's corner of Cherry Fork Cemetery. A couple of years later, on a hot August day in 1896, Maurice Hudson, a local farmer, noticed a strange sound passing Cherry Fork Cemetery. When he peered cautiously into the graveyard, his eyes opened wide. Over Roscoe Parker's grave, a ghostly man stood with arms outstretched and his hands spread wide. A stream of blood spurted from the neck, and atop the gushing blood was a head bouncing and bobbing.

For many years, people claimed to see balls of light flitting from grave to grave at Cherry Fork Cemetery near Winchester when they passed. And many refused to drive their carriages and cars along that route for fear of seeing a ghost.

Scioto County

Dead Man Hollow
Shawnee State Forest
13291 US-52 (State Forest Road 2)
West Portsmouth, Ohio 45633
38.698616, -83.237139

Dead Man Hollow—Tinker's Tale

Dead Man Hollow where a ghost vents out a ghastly howl.

A mysterious grave lies deep within a hollow near Portsmouth. It is in a dense, dark forest in a secluded pocket of Shawnee State Forest tucked between Little Gum Hollow and Webb Hollow on the right fork of Twin Creek. In the 1930s, CCC laborers working on the forest roadway found bones. Wedged within the crevice of a small rock overhang nearby were combs, implements, and tin plates—the type of things a peddler would trade along with the tools he would use for repairs around the remote homes he stopped in on his way. The remains were later moved and reburied adjacent to the little cleft in the rocks.

A stone was set along the right fork of Twin Creek in the hollow to commemorate the peddler. It read: "H. T. Aug. 13, 1824. A. D., Dead M." Upon finding the bones, old folks began to recall talk of a peddler who, in the 1820s, routinely visited the rural towns nearby and who had oddly ceased calling on farms on his usual route. They remembered hearing that a peddling tinker had paused in the village of Buena Vista in Scioto County along the Ohio River. After selling his wares, he was directed along a 6-hour rugged footpath northeast to the settlement of Upper Turkey Creek, a community about three miles north of the town of Friendship. Unfortunately, he never got to his destination.

The old stone marking the mysterious grave.

Most believed the peddler was ambushed and murdered, but no one knew the truth about how he died, or at least they would not tell. For many years, locals avoided the area of the hollow after dark reporting ghostly screams, whistling, and strange noises. After many years, floodwaters along the Twin Creek washed the grave away, and a bag of trinkets scattered nearby was discovered.

Scioto County

2nd Street (Between Market and Jefferson)
Portsmouth, Ohio 45662
38.731666, -83.004245

Front Street to Scioto Street
Portsmouth, Ohio 45662
38.730860, -83.007292

Washington, Ohio (Bridge)
Ohio 104 Portsmouth, Ohio 45662
38.733110, -83.011746

Woman in Black

The old Scioto Bridge where ghostly shenanigans occurred.

There was a ghost once walking the streets of Portsmouth. In July of 1888, Nat Smith and Joe Henry were working their way home from the market in downtown Portsmouth to Carey's Run a few miles west. It was about 10:00 p.m. As the two farmers strolled from Second Street to Front, they talked nervously about the recent murder of a man named Rayburn occurring near the Scioto Bridge. They were heading that route, the crime remained unsolved, and they surely did not want to be next.

As they chatted, a woman wearing a black dress and veil slipped past the two. The men eyed the scene, noting her steps were peculiarly silent and that she was clasping a baby tightly in her arms. Curious, they began to follow. Her progress was slow as she swept along the streets. When she reached the Scioto Bridge, the men felt an absolute dread overcome them. They paused, watching her stop in the center. Then she raised her arms into the air and tossed the tiny bundle into the water below. Nat and Joe's eyes followed the descent. They were too shaken to move. Oddly, there was no splash. The men snapped their eyes upward until they paused on the woman who had tossed her baby into the river. She turned, faced them, and lifted her veil. The sad face of a beautiful woman stared back at them before she completely disappeared.

More people saw this woman in black. Some believed she was the ghost of a woman who fell with her children into the river from the bridge when it collapsed a few years earlier. Others thought it could be a secretive woman who had stopped with a newborn at a local inn, then left suddenly without checking out. Others thought she was an omen of a murder to come.

The new Scioto Bridge where a ghostly woman in black walks.

Pike County

Pike Lake State Park
Pike Lake Road
Bainbridge, Ohio 45612
39.159920, -83.218545

The Haunted Stump

Pike Lake—where ghostly amputated hands rise up from a stump.

Long ago, when a farmer needed to clear land for a house or field, all the neighbors for miles around would come together and help out. They would cut the trees down to stumps, chop them into logs, and with handspikes, roll them into a pile, and have a bonfire. It was called a 'log rolling,' and it was a time of picnics and festivities for the whole community. Everyone took turns tending the fires, and once in a while, a spark would fly and a flame would lick the hem of a shirt or dress sending all into a frenzy to extinguish it.

At one particular log burning in the 1860s, where Pike Lake State Park is now, a young woman of about 18 years of age was working with the others poking and prodding the limbs and branches to keep the fire strong and the wood burning. She eased her way around one tall stack of fire, and a huge, flaming log broke loose from the top of the pile and careened downward. As she had her stick in her hand, the log rolled on it so the young woman keeled inward, and she could not release her fingers. She fell forward and was dragged to the earth until her palms slapped hard on the ground. The log rolled right over her hands and to her wrists.

Help came quickly, but not fast enough. The girl's hands were so severely burned, as she was wringing them, they fell right off and on to a stump. She died, and for years after, those passing the stump would see two charred ghost hands rising from the stump or feel their hot grasp on their ankles as they passed by.

Pike Lake trail—while walking the trails, watch for an old stump and ghostly hands wavering above it. Because if you pass it by unknowing, you may end up with a detached hand hitching a ride on your ankle. Yep, that is spooky.

Ross County

Mt. Union Pleasant Valley Cemetery
Union Lane
Chillicothe, Ohio 45601
39.390542, -83.052418

Elizabeth's Grave

Mt. Union Pleasant Valley Cemetery with hanging tree in the background. To the left are the drag marks made by the grave that was moved. No human tracks were found.

Elizabeth's headstone.

A curious legend at Mt. Union Pleasant Valley Cemetery is about a grieving woman named Elizabeth who hung herself on a tree in the cemetery after her husband died. The townspeople quickly recovered the corpse and buried her beneath the same tree in the rear of the cemetery. But, not long after, her ghost began to show itself in the misty evenings. Her headstone mysteriously works its way from the back of the cemetery and wanders to the front.

Montgomery County

Woodland Cemetery and Arboretum
*Boy and Dog Road
Dayton, Ohio 45409
Grave: 39.742451, -84.177362*

Johnny's Grave

Johnny's Grave at Woodland Cemetery and Arboretum showing the loyalty of a dog to a child even after death.

Five-year-old Johnny Morehouse (1855-1860) lived with his mother, Mary Margaret, and father, John, in the rear of the family cobbler shop along the Miami & Erie Canal near what is now Patterson Boulevard in Dayton. On a hot August 14th day in 1860, Johnny was playing along the canal. He fell into the dark depths, and his dog repeatedly tried to save him, but by the time he pulled the boy to the side of the canal, Johnny was dead.

After burying Johnny in Woodland Cemetery, his dog refused to leave his grave, staying by the young boy even after death. Stories tell of visitors to the cemetery who saw the dog and left treats and food for him. The tradition continues. Trinkets are left on the grave to honor the loyal pup. The ghost of Johnny and his dog play at the cemetery, and the dog's playful bark blends with his tiny owner's giggles in the night.

Visitors to Woodland Cemetery and Arboretum can find the graves of many famous Dayton natives including local newspaper columnist Erma Bombeck and pioneer aviators Orville Wright and Wilbur Wright. But the most sought after memorial is the grave of Johnny Morehouse.

Butler County

Intersections of Oxford Milford Road and Earhart Road
4253 Earhart Road
Oxford, Ohio 45056
39.560111,-84.702877

Oxford Light

The road where a ghostly light appears in the dead of night.

Two sweethearts would meet at night at the sharp curve where Oxford Milford and Earhart roads merge outside Oxford. He would park his motorcycle along Earhart Road, wait for the girl to signal three times with her car headlights, then flash the headlight on his motorcycle three times in return. One night, her parents caught her sneaking out, and she did not show. He waited, then angry, the young man raced away, failing to make the turn. He died. His ghost returns to wait for his girl. Those who park and flash their headlights three times have seen the motorcycle headlight making a quick run toward their car. Then it vanishes.

Butler County

Maud Hughes Road Bridge over Train Tracks
6385-6399 Maud Hughes Road
Liberty Township, Ohio 45044
39.394545,-84.410448

Screaming Bridge

Screaming Bridge—a legendary screamer lurks here.

Screaming Bridge used to be a lonely stretch of twisting backroads along Maud Hughes Road. Teens would come from West Chester or Fairfield, Maud, or Mason and park their cars along the old bridge passing over a railway. The driver would flip off the ignition while passengers slowly rolled down their windows. Then, in the silence, they would listen for the ghostly screams of a woman who had, after attempting to kill herself by jumping from the bridge, changed her mind. She caught herself on the guardrail, but a train came through, killing her while she dangled there. Now, her screams haunt the air.

Butler County

Hangman's Hollow
Hamilton Richmond Road
Hamilton, Ohio 45013
39.434520, -84.604321

The old hollow is about .4 mile from the intersection of Hamilton Richmond, Gardner and Old Oxford Roads

Dead Guardian of Hangman's Hollow

Darrtown Pike in earlier, more remote days and not far from Hangman's Hollow. *Photo Courtesy: Darrtown.com*

On October 2nd and 3rd of 1851, Butler County held its first official fair presented by the newly reorganized, state-authorized Agricultural Society. It was set up in a small grove of oaks near the Miami-Erie Canal just north of Hamilton. There were no racetracks, no carnies selling games, and no 4-H kids displaying their projects. Instead, there were exhibits, including samples of this year's summer harvests, farm implements, and animals like horses, cattle, and pigs.

It would not appear much by today's standards. But to four wide-eyed country boys between the ages of eight to twelve hailing from the village of Darrtown, it was exciting enough to grab up their horses and head the long trip to Hamilton about nine miles away. Twelve-year-old Taylor Marshall was the ringleader of the group. Along with him rode 8-year-old Ben Scott, 10-year-old Chambers Flenner, and 11-year-old Dan Warwick.

Four boys from Darrtown met their fears at Hangman's Hollow.

The boys enjoyed the day at the fair, and as evening came to pass, they realized they had lost track of time. Deep into autumn, their return route was along Darrtown Pike—now Hamilton Richmond Road. It was a path thick with ghastly, gnarly-limbed, leafless trees, and an isolated dip in the dusty road where 22 years earlier in July of 1829, Martin Koble from Lancaster, Pennsylvania found the secluded pocket and hanged himself there. He was a stranger in town, and no one knew why he committed such a deed. But it took two years even to find his next of kin. Between then and the time the boys traveled through this little pocket of scary, it had gotten quite a reputation as a haven for robbers and ruffians and some thought, a ghost or two. Worse yet, its nickname was Hangman's Hollow.

The boys dreaded the little section just outside the city, even if they did not like to make a show of it. Once in a while, one or the other would mutter something brave like, "There ain't no such thing as ghosts" or "I ain't afraid of nothin'." It only seemed to make it worse as they worked their way about a mile and a half outside the town and the road began to lead slowly into the dreaded hollow. The air was dark and crisp as they descended into the valley. It was then they heard whispers and ran into a crowd of people in the roadway staring into the woods. Curiously, the four dismounted and scurried along the hollow, following the pointing fingers through the old creek bed until they came to a halt. A farmer, searching for his lost pigs, came upon a body. It was a man hanging with suspenders around his neck over the creek. There he dangled right in front of the boys. His face was blackened and distorted as if pecked and nibbled by birds, animals, and insects. It was a stockman who left the fair with a purse full of cash. He had been ambushed, dragged into the hollow, and killed for the loot.

He was later buried in a shallow grave where Gardner Road is today. His skeleton was found in the early 1900s by workers digging a culvert. His ghost shows up to some traveling the route, a shadowy figure rising at the dip where the land slopes downward. Be wary if you see him. The spirit once warned unsuspecting travelers of outlaws hiding in the secluded woods, ready to ambush them for money.

Hangman's Hollow today.

Preble County

Preble County District Library— Eaton Branch

301 N Barron Street
Eaton, Ohio 45320
39.746333, -84.637343

Lida Griswold –Ghostly Librarian

The original Eaton Public Library as it appeared when Lida Griswold worked and died there. *Courtesy: Columbus Metropolitan Library.*

On July 8th, 1909, 37-year-old Lida Griswold was alone in the library with her 13-year-old son, Cloyd, and her sister. There was one patron left in the room, a gentleman who had slipped quietly into the library and was reading a book. As it was closing time, Missus Griswold arose and made the customary announcement that the library was closing, and all patrons must leave.

The man stood and began walking toward her with a gun in his hand. He declared he would end it all, shot her, and then turned the gun on himself. He killed Lida Griswold. Her family buried her in the local graveyard, Mound Cemetery. Her perpetrator, a married man by the name of Henry Rife, only grazed his skin. He was executed for his crime in 1910.

Lida and the old library may be gone, but her spirit is not. Occasionally, she lets visitors to the newer library (built overtop the old location and where the murder took place) know she is still keeping an eye out on those who enter. Books will topple from a shelf when no live person is nearby. Hushed chatter is heard in the room when no one else but the listener is there.

The Eaton Public Library today.

Warren County

Kings Island—Dog Street Cemetery
Kings Island Drive
Maineville, Ohio 45039
39.350226,-84.267793

The Ghostly Walk of Missouri Jane

Dog Street Cemetery. Beyond, Kings Island. Haunted by a ghost.

There are 81 known burials in Dog Street Cemetery located in the parking lot of Kings Island. It originated in 1803 and is the eternal resting place of the Baysores and the Dills. Most lived to a ripe old age of 60 or 70, but others like Missouri Jane Galeenor died young. Some believe Missouri is the little ghost girl wandering the cemetery. Kings Island opened in 1972, but for well over a half-century before that, people have reported the ghostly apparition of a child in a blue dress working her way among the graves.

Hamilton County

Darby-Lee Historic Cemetery
5999 Bender Road
Cincinnati, Ohio 45233
39.099760, -84.653758

Legend of the Fiddler Green

Darby-Lee Cemetery—Mister Darby still walks the tall hill that overlooks the Ohio River, but in ghostly form. He lights his lantern and plays his fiddle to signal safety to escaping slaves.

Darby-Lee Cemetery lies in the woodland overlooking the Ohio River in Delhi Township of Cincinnati. On certain nights, a green light floats up along the tombstones at this aged little graveyard. The eerie sound of fiddle rolls along the green grass which nearly hides the graves before the tune wafts on past toward the river.

It is small, protected by an old wooden fence, and has about seventeen ancient gravestones surrounding a pale obelisk in the middle. This center monument, grayed with age, belongs to the landowner Henry Darby, an avid abolitionist. During the early 1800s, Mister Darby would walk to the tall hill that overlooked the Ohio River below, light his lantern, and play his fiddle to signal safety to the escaping slaves crossing over the river from Kentucky. Not long after his death and burial, at the very place he summoned so many to safety, people began to see the glow of his lantern bobbing around the cemetery. They would hear the ghostly, shrill sounds of his fiddle sweeping between the hills and down to the river, still beckoning those below it was safe to cross.

Darby-Lee Cemetery and just beyond, the Ohio River.

Greene County

Clifton Gorge State Nature Preserve
Yellow Springs, Ohio 45387
Parking off Jackson Street:
39.794942, -83.828476
Walk Gorge Trail less than a mile to
Blue Hole: 39.795109, -83.839102

Spirit of Blue Hole

Blue Hole at Clifton Gorge—it has a legend steeped in history.

Long ago, there was an Indian woman whose tribe lived near the location of Clifton Gorge State Nature Preserve today. She was in love with a man from her tribe. However, he loved another. One afternoon as many young men and women gathered for an outing along the pretty valley where the Little Miami waters flow blue and deep, she watched as a rival flirted playfully with her love. The man she loved, he flirted in return.

In a fit of jealousy, the young woman decided to force the man to choose her over the rival. She would hurl herself from the wall to the waters below. He would certainly see her falling, turn his back on the flirting woman, and rush to save her.

Thus, she clambered up to the highest rock, screamed into the air to catch his attention, then jumped. Instead of running to save her, the man turned to the young woman he had been chatting with and let his young admirer drown. Now, there are times when the evening turns its back to the day sky, and when the moon lights up the valley, you can see the young woman standing atop the rock. Her ghostly screams fill the air before she disappears into the blue waters below.

Blue Hole at Clifton Gorge is about a mile walk with steps from the parking lot (1-way) along the Gorge Trail and beside the Little Miami River. You will see it as a deep pool not long after Steamboat Rock.

Miami County

Fort Piqua Plaza Banquet Center
308 N Main Street
Piqua, Ohio 45356
40.148981, -84.240114

Old Building Full of Old Ghosts

Fort Piqua Plaza—A new life, same old ghosts.

Fort Piqua Hotel was constructed in 1891 reputedly as a payback from a feud with rival Troy after they trashed Piqua to gain the county seat and courthouse in the mid-1800s. Piqua outshined Troy by building Fort Piqua Hotel that takes up almost an entire city block. Now it is Fort Piqua Plaza Banquet Center, with a new makeover and housing restaurants, pubs, and even a public library. Between, though, is when it picked up a few ghosts—a handyman who died in 1910, a worker killed during the construction, and a porter crushed to death in an elevator, to name a few. Oh, and ghostly music sweeps out into the hallways from an old dining area.

Miami County

Duncan Mourning Chair
The Fletcher Cemetery
8201-8269 Co Hwy 22
Fletcher, Ohio 45326
40.147040, -84.111300

The Devil's Chair

Mourning chair at Fletcher Cemetery. Would you sit in it? And if you did, would you see a ghost appear?

Mourning chairs were not uncommon in cemeteries in the 1800s as a place for loved ones to sit while visiting a grave. The Duncan family has one at Fletcher Cemetery. Some call these chairs Haunted Chairs or Devil's Chairs, and urban legends maintain sitting on one can conjure up all sorts of mischief, tomfoolery, and trouble—like seeing a ghost once you settle in on the seat. Please be kind if you challenge this legend, these monuments are old—treat them like your favorite recliner at home!

Darke County

Bear's Mill
6450 Arcanum Bears Mill Road
Greenville, Ohio 45331
40.106824, -84.542057

Spirited Footsteps at Bear's Mill

Bear's Mill in Greenville has a dead, old owner who just does not want to leave this world.

Gabriel Baer opened this water-operating gristmill in 1850, and it was in operation until the 1970s. Now it is run by a volunteer group, Friends of Bear's Mill. The original owner haunts the building. When it is quiet, you can hear his ghostly footsteps padding along on the floors.

Champaign County

Old Railway Tracks in Urbana
Ohio Bicycle Route 3
Urbana, Ohio 43078
40.114926, -83.751634

Lincoln Ghost Train

The train that carried the body of Abraham Lincoln across the United States has been seen as a phantom train complete with ghostly, pale faces staring out the windows. *Image: Library of Congress*

Do not forget to mark April 29th on your calendar as the date the nine-car Lincoln ghost train wanders down the same tracks in Urbana that the actual train took on the same day in 1865. One week after President Lincoln's assassination on April 14th, 1865, the funeral train carrying his body weaved its way across the northern United States toward Springfield, Illinois for burial.

It made frequent stops along the way. It was not merely to allow mourners to pay respects to the late president along the 13-day trip. There were layovers often to freshen the flowers surrounding the corpse to keep the smell of rotting flesh to a minimum. As the train progressed along its route, one of the places it trudged through was Urbana on Saturday, April 29th at 10:40 p.m. Thousands showed up to see the train pass.

You can watch for the ghost train from the Simon Kenton Trail, a hike/bike path in Urbana. Public Parking for Trail Access: Depot Coffee House, 644 Miami St, Urbana, Ohio 43078 (40.109011, -83.759691)

Nowadays, a few folks show up for another reason. Legends say that on April 29th, a ghostly funeral car carrying the body of President Lincoln makes its way along the tracks through Urbana on this special anniversary date. Some have seen it shrouded in black with a skeletal crew within, while others have seen mysterious lights that vanish into nothingness. Those with homes near the tracks have awakened to the sound of a ghostly train rambling along the railroad. The spectral scream of the whistle sweeps along the railway, and legends persist that clocks throughout town stop for 20 minutes, the same amount of time Lincoln's funeral train stopped in this pretty village.

Fayette County

Cherry Hill
OH-38 and Co Hwy 113
Yatesville, Ohio 43106
39.665178,-83.441091 to
39.682784,-83.415291

Headless Horseman of Cherry Hill

A headless horseman was seen along the roads of Yatesville.

A headless horseman once stalked residents along State Route 38 near Yatesville. One pair of early tavernkeepers living on a small rise called Cherry Hill were notorious counterfeiters and ruffians. When a ghostly horseman began to show on the hill near their home, rumors wafted through the community that the innkeepers had murdered a federal agent secretly investigating their illegal activities. The husband killed the federal agent, cut off his head, and dumped his body in a well. They found his horse tied to a tree. When the wife discovered her husband had murdered the man, he tried to kill her too. She turned him into the police. Many years later, when a farmer was plowing, several skeletons were found on Cherry Hill where the inn once stood and the dead horseman rode.

Highland County

Fallsville Wildlife Area
10211 Careytown Road
New Vienna, Ohio 45159
Parking: 39.285561, -83.630011
Old Homestead: 39.286057, -83.632949

Fallsville Christmas Ghost

Fallsville—once a mill town, it is now Fallsville Wildlife Area and a ghost town—with a ghost. That you can visit.

One chilly Christmas Eve in the 1880s, two sisters living alone in an isolated pocket of Highland County heard a rap-rap upon their door. Few people were remaining in the tiny town that once surrounded their home. On a wintery Christmas Eve, they questioned who would dare to brave the weather and visit. They arose to part the curtains and peered out the window into the snowy night.

Beneath a moon and at the end of their walkway, there stood an Indian in full dress. Intrigued and with wide eyes, they watched his mouth moving as if trying to form words. His fingers were weaving in sign language. But unable to hear his words nor understand the sign language, they did not know what he wanted from them. Before the two could decide to open the door or not, he vanished. This mysterious apparition came each Christmas after that. The two women hired an interpreter to read the hand signs, and from that deciphering, they found that there was tribal treasure buried on the property, and he had come to claim it.

The road to Fallsville. The house was to the left around the bend.

The story would travel around the broader community, along with many rumors of witchcraft and ghosts. Many knew the women well. The two sisters were the daughters of Simon and Elizabeth Clouser, who bought and settled on a couple of parcels of land along the waterfalls of Clear Creek many years earlier. The property came with an 1812 two-story stone home initially built by a John Timberlake, who had recorded the town around him as Fallsville in 1848.

Its industry was a grist mill built by the waterfall with Simon's hands. There was a church, a cemetery, and five small blocks of streets with about eight homes across the creek. Hoping to gain status as the county seat, the town hardly grew above six families, one of them Simon's own with three children: Susanna, Charlotte, and Lewis. Although Lewis would eventually move away to New York and the elderly parents would pass away, the two Clouser sisters lived out their days quietly in the home and were among the last citizens of the community.

Standing where the ghost once stood on Christmas Eve. The pile of bricks and stone is pretty much all remaining of the home.

They were somewhat eccentric—the siblings lived alone in the old stone home, did not come out often, and were easy prey to gossip. The Christmas ghost story lent credence to more strange rumors surrounding the two. Some said they clung to old superstitions and would greet strangers once in a while visiting the falls along Clear Creek. As the visitors walked away, the sisters threw salt at their feet to protect the town from evil.

Little remains of Fallsville except for a mark on the map, some steps slightly visible by the falls, and the Methodist Church and cemetery. The house was torn down around the 1970s, but a bit of the old Clouser home where the Indian visited remains. The ghost of the Indian still visits the wildlife area land owned by the State of Ohio. Music has been heard in the tiny woodlots and meadows, the sound of an Indian bell making an eerie call out for those who might still find his treasure. On some evenings before Christmas Day, he is seen standing on the path in front of the heap of the old home still trying to claim his tribal treasures.

Remnants of a ghost town's past—a quarry—hidden in the forest and a bit of fog rolling in.

You can visit the remains of the Clouser homestead at Fallsville Wildlife Area, park in the small lot, and walk the roadway back. It is a beautiful hike and not scary at all. If you walk the short dirt road and stop at the open area and look to the left, you can see where the Clouser home used to be and perhaps see the ghost. Take the trail farther, and you can see the waterfall and ponds. It is a wildlife area, so you must follow the rules and watch out for hunters!

Clinton County

Wilmington College—College Hall
College Street
Wilmington, Ohio 45177
39.444827,-83.818229

Spirited Horse

College Hall—where a ghostly horse is heard.

Quakers established Wilmington College in 1870, led by Civil War Colonel Azariah Doan. College Hall was the first building opened in 1871, offering a diversity of uses—from a dorm for faculty/staff to a public meeting place. It also housed the skeleton of Azariah Doan's beloved horse, Old Bill. Brought to the college after the Civil War, the horse became a big part of memorial ceremonies. After it died, the college displayed the entire skeleton for many years, but later, only the skull was left out to view. Students relate that the horse's ghost returns, and its hooves clomp along the hallways at night.

Clark County

George Rogers Clark Park
Daniel Hertzler House Museum
5072-5098 Lower Valley Pike,
Springfield, Ohio 45506
39.909216, -83.911192

Ghost of the Richest Man in Town

Daniel Hertzler, left, haunts his old home where he was murdered, above.

Watch for him peering out the window.

Daniel Hertzler was an early Mennonite settler from Pennsylvania who prospered as a businessman in Clark County—including being the president of the Clark County Bank. Along with his wife, Catherine, and ten children, he built a farm, sawmills, and even a brick distillery.

Hertzler owned a large house on a property overlooking a village once belonging to native Shawnee, now the George Rogers Clark Park. The family was worth quite a bit for the times, and many believed Hertzler kept much of his cash at his home.

On a chilly October night in 1867, robbers broke into 67-year-old Daniel Hertzler's home. His wife had arisen to care for a sick child and heard strange sounds. She awakened Hertzler, and he made his way toward the noises. Only moments later, the surprised robbers would be making their way to Springfield with Hertzler's horse and buggy. Hertzler lay dead on the floor.

None of the men suspected of robbing Daniel Hertzler's home and murdering him faced prosecution. Police caught two suspicious characters, but they escaped. No one paid for the wicked deeds they had done. Hertzler was buried in Ferncliff Cemetery in Springfield beneath a tall monument bearing his name. It is quiet there, the birds sing soft songs in the summer, and the wind blows gently across the freshly mowed lawn. Not so in the place that he called home. His corpse might be in the quiet of the cemetery, but his spirit haunts his old house overlooking the old Shawnee Village. His face is seen at a window gazing out to the lawn, looking for the men who murdered him and waiting for their return so he can give them their due.

Southeastern Ohio

Perry County

Otterbein United Methodist Church Cemetery
County Road 62/ Otterbein Road NW
Rushville, Ohio 43150
39.77194, -82.36333

Bloody Horseshoe Grave

Bloody Horseshoe Grave Cemetery—sometimes your actions come back to haunt you.

James Kennedy Henry was a farmer and early settler born in 1814. In 1844, two women caught his eye—Mary Angle and Rachael Hodge. Both were attractive and charming, and James was so smitten with both, he could not decide which one to marry. One night while heading home from visiting his sweethearts, he fell to sleep on the saddle of his horse. When he awakened, the horse was standing outside the door of Mary Angle.

James took it as a sign—fate had decided Mary would be his bride. The two were married on a chilly day in January 1844. It was a tradition for the parents of the bride and groom to give them a gift they could use in their new life as a couple. Such, the newlyweds received one handsome workhorse from Mary's parents and one workhorse from James' parents, so the two had a team of horses to start a farm.

Mary and James were happy together for a little more than a year until Mary died giving birth to their first child. In February of 1845, James buried her in a corner plot at the local Otterbein Cemetery. Distraught, the widowed man would do everything he could to forget Mary—throwing himself into his farming trying desperately to rebuild his life. But there was one thing James did not do. He did not return the horse that Mary's parents had given the couple on their wedding day.

James took three years before courting his earlier sweetheart, Rachael Hodge. During this time, in the surrounding area, some whispered that James had broken tradition by not returning the horse to Mary's parents after she died. Mary's family was having a difficult time making ends meet and needed the horse for their farm. There were hard feelings between the families not spoken aloud.

Rachael was only 22-years-old when she took James' hand in marriage. All would seem perfect except for one small detail occurring when James visited his first wife's grave not long after taking his new bride. He noted on the back of Mary's headstone, the bloody red shape of a horseshoe! It was an omen that would always linger in the back of his mind for many years. James and Rachael had four daughters and were married for nearly 11 years. Happy, the couple were, but the dark cloud of the horseshoe grave followed James wherever he went.

Then the inevitable happened. The curse would come full swing. While working in the barn one Friday evening, he was kicked in the head by a horse and instantly killed. It was the very horse James had not returned to Mary's parents that put him in the grave. To this day, the bloody horseshoe print is still marking the grave.

Bloody Horseshoe Grave.

Perry County

Old Rainer Road
Co Road 3
Roseville, Ohio 43777
39.802068, -82.128731

The Headless Ghost Rider Mounted on a Piebald Steed on a Lonely Road between Roseville and Saltillo

Old Rainer Road where a headless ghost rider was witnessed.

Old Rainer Road between Saltillo and Roseville is a lonely one and has been for a long time. Still, since the early 1800s, travelers along this route have reported seeing a ghostly piebald horse with a white mane and tail. On its back, a headless horseman rode. He wore a buckskin hunting shirt and leggings and carried a rifle over his right shoulder.

A traveling salesman saw it. But, of course, nobody believed him. Then, 87-year-old William Dunn, a minister, and 46-year-old John Tanner, a butcher, saw the apparition in June of 1888. The two neighbors were returning home in the dark sometime before midnight. The headless horseman ran between the men, spooking both their horses. Dunn and Tanner related the story a few times to family before deciding it was in the best interest of their reputations to keep quiet about their bizarre adventure.

Still, many old-timers knew where the story had begun. A wealthy man had stopped at a local cabin around 1812, just off the same road Dunn and Tanner had ridden. The traveler was murdered in his sleep; his head was ripped from his body with a blunt ax. Not long after the body was found, those passing along the same route began seeing a headless man mounted on a piebald horse cantering beside them. The murderer, who lived nearby, was driven insane by the nightly visits of the ghost and drowned himself in a creek.

The loot was found in the murderer's cabin. The townspeople in the surrounding community worried the booty was cursed, buried the ill-gotten money in a secret place, and vowed never to tell anyone where it was hidden. For years, the headless horseman disappeared, and the story was nearly forgotten. Then travelers, including the salesman, Dunn and Tanner, and other wayfarers, saw the ghostly figure. Many believed that the murdered man's money had been found after many years, the secret where it was buried revealed. Such, the ghost had come back to haunt the highway until his possessions were returned.

Vinton County

Moonville Tunnel
Along Moonville Rail Trail
Hope-Moonville Road
McArthur, Ohio 45651
Parking: 39.308325, -82.324495
Tunnel: 39.307389, -82.322434

The Ghost of Moonville

Moonville Tunnel

Theodore Lawhead was an engineer for the Marietta and Cincinnati railroad company that ran through southeastern Ohio towns like Marietta, Chillicothe, Kings Station, Ingham Station, and Moonville. The route he took cut a path through Ohio's wildest terrains and had many tunnels and trestles. Both eastbound and westbound trains shared a single track with passing areas.

One November night in 1880, while Lawhead was heading through southern Ohio, the dispatch failed to notify the eastbound train of the westbound's route and time. The two collided near Moonville Tunnel, and Lawhead and his fireman died instantly. After the wreck, many of the trainmen feared going along that stretch of the railroad. They said they would see the flicker of lantern light when they came along a certain section of the tracks near the tunnel in Moonville. As they got closer, a robed figure would join the flicker of lantern light and step out toward the train before vanishing.

He was gone, but his story would live on because Lawhead returned. A February 1895 Chillicothe Gazette wrote the following: *The ghost of Moonville, after an absence of one year, has returned and is again at its old pranks, haunting B&O S-W freight trains and their crews. Monday night the ghost appeared just east of the cut, which is one half mile the other side of Moonville. It showed up in front of fast freight No. 99 west bound, which is due at Moonville at 8:50 p.m.*

The train was hauled by engine 226, in charge of Engineer William Washburn. The conductor was Mr. Charles Bazler. The ghost was attired in a pure white robe, and carried a lantern. It had a flowing white beard, its eyes glistened like balls of fire, and surrounding it was a halo of twinkling stars. As the train approached, the lantern was swung across the track—

It is just a short hike from the parking lot to the tunnel; I am walking through the parking lot in this picture. For those with wheelchairs, it has a pebbled path. You can see the tunnel just beyond the bridge.

Even though the trains are long gone, folks still dread taking this path. It is remote. And the ghost of Engineer Lawhead continues to be seen at Moonville Tunnel. Maybe you can see him too. There is a rail-trail going through the tunnel you can hike if you are not too scared to take the route the ghost traveled.

My ghostly Moonville picture taken when no one else was around.

Hocking County

Hocking Hills State Park
Old Man's Cave
19852 OH-664
Logan, Ohio 43138
39.435351, -82.541179

The Legend of Old Man's Cave

Old Man's Cave at Hocking Hills State Park is home to the ghost of a hermit named Retzler and his dog. Although some have perpetuated the name of Richard Roe, the term *Richard Roe* is a fictitious name given in legal proceedings when a true name is unknown much like John Doe is the given name for an unidentified corpse in the medical industry. Richard Roe is believed to have been falsely bequeathed in the 1970s before research was done for the correct name linked with the legend.

The oldest known legend of Old Man's Cave was reported in newspapers in 1907. Two boys were exploring the caves near Cedar Grove and not far from Logan. After a while, they grew tired and built a small fire on a ledge inside a large recess cave. They were talking about their adventures of the day while the low flame danced above the kindling they had collected.

Upon hearing a rustling in the leaves akin to footsteps, they paused to look up and were startled by the image of an older man. He had stopped near the fire, appearing quite curious about their chitchat. The boys were also mystified by his peculiar appearance—he had a long gray beard and old-fashioned clothing of leather, including moccasins on his feet. He had a gun slung over his shoulder. Nearby, a huge, white hound had stopped beside him. The old man slipped quietly past as if he did not want to alarm them, and eventually disappeared into the hazy darkness of the far side of the cave, seeming to sink into the sandy ground.

Quite unsettled, the boys ran home to their families and told them of the ghostly man who had appeared to them in the cave. Immediately, curious villagers bearing picks and shovels went to the cave and began to draw out the dirt where the old man disappeared. The ground appeared sunken into a room about four feet square. Within and about three feet down, they discovered a box. As they lifted the lid, they found the mummified remains of a man and a dog, almost as lifelike as if they had just crawled inside. There were also cooking utensils, a flintlock gun, and a pot with information about the old man's life. He was a trapper along the Cedar Valley Creek who died in 1777. Although the old man's name was Retzler, and the name of his dog was Harper, and his gun, Pointer, most will know him as The Old Man of Old Man's Cave.

The park is open dawn to dusk, so you cannot go there at night. Even today, some claim to see him moseying along the trail during daylight hours with his dog. Throughout the years, many have seen his ghostly figure with a baying hound in the misty air of dawn.

Hocking County

Scotts Creek Falls
13843 State Route 93
Logan, Ohio 43138
39.532216, -82.420650

Awful Calamity at Scotts Creek—Death Hole

The Death Hole coughs up ghosts once in a while that it has swallowed up in the past.

It was a Tuesday morning deep in the summer of 1887 when 29-year-old Johannes Bensonhafer loaded his wagon with twenty bushels of wheat to deliver to the local mill in Logan. Along with him was Johannes' new wife, 19-year-old Clara. They had been married a little shy of six months. Once settled into the wagon, the two traveled along what is now a part of State Route 93 but was then called Scotts Creek Road. At just about 10:25 a.m., they passed the ford along Scotts Creek and headed a little farther past a layer of stones called 'The Falls' along the left side of the road.

A man following in a carriage watched the couple pass the ford as he continued onward just a short way. Suddenly, he heard a loud clatter and the scream of horses forcing him to turn his carriage around. He found the team of horses that had been pulling the Bensonhafer wagon struggling hard in a deep pool of water. Johannes and Clara had vanished, but a hat and basket were floating near the surface. Tiny bubbles gurgled from somewhere below.

For unknown reasons, Johannes had turned the wagon along a deep section of water that local legend held was a nearly bottomless passage beneath the falls called Death Hole. Most likely, the man driving the wagon had no clue a 12-foot drop lay hidden beneath the water. He had innocently urged his horses forward. They had plunged downward along with the cart laden with wheat. Clara and Johannes were pitched forward and tossed like ragdolls into the water.

The young couple and their team of horses were pulled too late from the water. They lay the corpses of Clara and Johannes on the bank, waiting for the coroner. It was not long before crowds came to see the dead couple lying there in a state that described them as seeming to appear as if they had fallen asleep on the bank, complete with rosy color still upon their cheeks.

The family buried the couple in nearby Ewing, and local newspapers would deem the tragedy the 'Awful Calamity' at Scotts Creek. Folks talked about the couple's sad demise for years. Then, that news faded away. But the Bensonhafers, do not rest. On some nights, you can hear the wagon along the road followed by muffled chatter of the young couple as their ghostly wagon slips toward the bank near the falls. Then there are the screams of horses as the phantom team descends into the murky depths of Scotts Creek and disappears.

Athens County

Athens Asylum—The Ridges of Ohio University
100 Ridges Circle
Athens, Ohio 45701
Asylum: 39.320380, -82.109311
Old Cemetery 1: 39.321999, -82.113851

Athens Asylum for the Insane

Athens Asylum—ghosts, inside and out. Now, tours focus on the history and not necessarily on the spiritual activity within. You can walk the grounds outside and still get a feel for spirits along the many trails and a couple asylum cemeteries nearby.

The old Athens Asylum is a familiar sight in the college town of Athens. Driving along the James A. Rhodes Appalachian Highway, it is easy to pick out the brick buildings just across the Hocking River and still standing on The Ridges, a wooded hillside just outside the town proper. It has been a solid fixture in the region for over 140 years— the building was a mental hospital from 1874 until 1993.

Now it is called Lin Hall and houses the Kennedy Art Museum for Ohio University. The building and grounds have been a great source for ghost stories over the years.

Building 26 was located on the hilltop. Touted by horror adventurers as the building for the criminally insane, it actually housed patients with Tuberculosis. It is gone. (39.323095, -82.113269)

Sometime long ago, I was driving my daughter and two of her friends home from a football game in town. At the time, you could visit the old asylum grounds after dark, and it was a rite of passage for high-schoolers to drive a certain brick drive leading uphill and passing an asylum cemetery before the road circled in front of old Building 26 that was touted to once house the criminally insane. There was but one way in and one way out. It was the practice to turn out the lights, making your way slowly around the circle before coming to a stop in front of the building.

One ghost story that stood out among others included the evil spirit of a criminal who would attack the vehicles. He would do all those horrifying things ghosts do to frightened teens in horror films. At the time, I believe, this ghost also sported a chainsaw. While he subdued those in the vehicle, the dead arose from the cemetery below to help. They dragged those within the car into the forest beyond.

Although we did not know it at the time, we would come face to face with this evil entity that very evening.

It was late at night and Halloween time, and I had just passed the main drive leading up to the asylum. A hushed conversation in the back seat of my car became quite heated. I peered into the rearview mirror as I had heard part of the discussion that went something like this— "So just ask her to drive up there. I won't let anything happen to us." The voice was deep, so I recognized it as the boyfriend of my daughter's friend—a high school football player who was still a bit haughty and high from a winning game that night. I looked into the rearview, saw all three faces looking up to me with cagey eyes. "You know I could hear the entire conversation; I'm two feet away in a closed compartment," I piped up. "But, sure, I will drive you up to the asylum." I did not mind. I thought that surely, it would be better an adult drove them up there than the three teens taking an unsupervised trip that might end like one of those horror movies. Since I missed the main entrance, I took a side drive.

As my car crept up the old path, the football player, who was sitting in the center of the backseat, threw a protective arm around my daughter and then one around her friend and grinned. I heard him cooing to them like he had a semi-automatic weapon tucked into his t-shirt to fight off whatever bad thing was ahead. We rolled the windows down as we passed the main administrative building, then several living quarters. The air in the car grew oppressive as we bumped along the raggedy brick road past the old cemetery. It was silent, *too* silent. We reached the peak of the hill, and my daughter advised me to turn off the lights, cruise slowly along the road, and upon reaching a certain point to stop and turn off the car. I did and began to park when I saw something move. "What is that—?" I started, interrupted by a loud grind of a chainsaw.

In less time than it took for me to gasp a breath, the car was surrounded by an army of blood-dripping creatures running feverishly with a chainsaw-wielding, wild-eyed beast of a man at their heels. A scream slipped up from the backseat of my car. I watched as the boy in the back, who had only moments earlier been a fearless seasoned warrior preparing for battle, peeled back his lips in a high-pitched cry and dove to the car floor. He abandoned the two girls desperately trying to roll up their windows and yelling for me to—"Drive! Drive! Drive!" I could not drive away as we were surrounded by figures everywhere.

What I did not know for probably the most horrifying four minutes of my life was that one of the fraternities had set up a haunted trail for different groups of students. I had taken a little-used backway onto the asylum grounds, and we had happened upon it quite by accident on both sides. The fraternity thought I was the first car of their reserved groups to get there that night. They got a test drive, and we got the scare of our lives. And I do believe that my daughter's friend stopped dating that boy the next day.

The building was eventually torn down. But others remain, including a section holding the traces of patient Margaret Schilling who accidentally locked herself in a room, unknown by staff, and died. Her corpse left a perfect impression of her body after it was found and taken away.

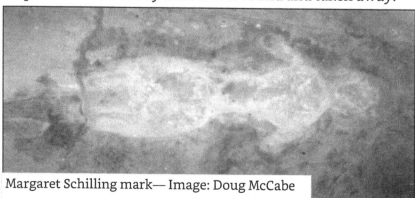

Margaret Schilling mark— Image: Doug McCabe

Athens County

Mustapha Island
View from Ohio Side:
Coolville, Ohio 45723
39.213080, -81.729950

Little Lights on Mustapha Island

The Kanawha along the Ohio River in 1907. *West Virginia and Regional History Center, West Virginia University Libraries.*

The steamer Kanawha left Pittsburgh on January 4th, 1916. It was just getting dark, and the air was frigid. Although the Ohio River was running high and fast, she had an experienced crew, and nothing appeared amiss. The boat had just gotten overhauled and was running smoothly. The only thing she lacked was a lifeboat removed less than a month earlier. She stopped at the wharf boat in Marietta 172 miles later to unload and load cargo. The wharf boat owner was Henry Best at the time. He demanded Captain Brady Berry deliver two barrels of lubricating oil to Little Hocking. Brady tried to appeal to the man's better senses; the water was dangerously high, and high wind was already putting a strain on the boat and crew. There was also construction in the process at Lock 19. Best refused to take no for an answer.

View from the Ohio side of Mustapha Island where twinkling lights were seen after the wreck of Steamboat Kanawha.

The second clerk on the Kanawha was a man by the name of Fred Hoyt. As they moored near the landing, he saw his mother in the crowd watching the boat, and she hailed him down. He quickly got off the steamer to greet her, and she pulled him aside and told her son she had a premonition of grave danger if the Kanawha was to continue on its journey. Although he contemplated she might be right, he had no choice but to board the steamer and resume onward.

From Marietta, they worked their way along on a blustery evening to Parkersburg. There, the cook refused to go farther and took off toward the train depot. By 7:00 p.m. on January 5th, they were coming up to Little Hocking, and the current was so strong, she went broadside to the waves. Lock 19 was submerged entirely, which the boat could have navigated past, but not so with the light towers on either side. Although prepared to cross safely, the hull rammed into a barely submerged steel light tower at the lock, leaving a gaping hole in the boat.

In moments, the steamer sunk to her roof. Fred Hoyt was able to climb to the rooftop with the help of four other crewmen. It was too late for four women he had seen while he was scurrying to safety and who were too far away to help. Those trapped in the lower areas of the Kanawha drowned. The crew and surviving passengers crowded around what boat floated until it rammed into Mustapha Island 2 miles away. Sixteen people died.

The wreck of the Steamboat Kanawha. Courtesy Cincinnati Library.

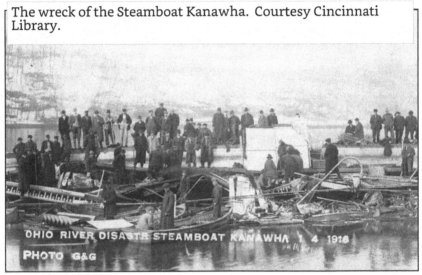

OHIO RIVER DISASTR STEAMBOAT KANAWHA 4 1918
PHOTO G&G

85-year-old Captain Cross and his first mate on the steamer Reuben Dunbar were the first to see the ghost lights flashing on and off and hovering around Mustapha Island downstream from the lock where the tragic accident occurred not long after the wreck. He gave the signal to land, believing someone was waving an emergency lantern, and the boat swung to the island shore. No one was on the island. Other steamboat captains following the river began seeing the yellowish glow of lantern there. The lights bounced all around the island into the 1930s. A Pittsburgh Press newspaper in August of 1939 noted that passengers on the Gordon C. Greene steamer were still seeing the lights each night while they passed by the island as shafts appearing like a flashlight, torch, or man carrying a lantern.

Meigs County

Sliding Hill

West Virginia Route 62
Hartford City, West Virginia
38.999546, -81.985601
View from Syracuse, Ohio:
38.998172, -81.980274

Ghostly Lantern Lights on Sliding Hill

Sliding Hill in West Virginia and right across the river from Syracuse in Meigs County where the lights were seen.

Just across the Ohio River from Syracuse, Ohio, there are two West Virginia towns. One is Hartford City, and the other is New Haven. Hartford City and New Haven are nearly back to back, about a mile and a half apart. You could probably stand between the two towns along West Virginia Route 62 that runs through both and yell loud enough for somebody to hear you across the river in Syracuse.

There between the two West Virginia towns is a place called Sliding Bend Hill or, for short, Sliding Hill—a sheer-edged hill that dips downward and causes the river to come together at nearly right angles. This awkward angle made it a dangerous bend for steamboat pilots as the water hit the rocks with such speed that it was difficult to navigate.

This dark recess had a ghost. Boatmen on the river and people traveling the roadways beside the river in Ohio and West Virginia reported seeing little lights dancing, ghosts, and even skeletons along Sliding Hill as far back as the late 1700s. In 1910, a family traveling south along the river in their houseboat anchored opposite Sliding Hill, unknowing of the mysterious lights. As dusk settled in the skies, the father began to see a strange light bobbing up and down the hillside. He grew suspicious of the light, silently slipped a skiff into the water, and paddled across. When he reached a position in the shadows, his eyes fell on a horrifying sight. He saw a huge headless monster shoving its weight into several large stones on the hillside just a short distance away. He made a hasty return, and in the dark of night, the family fled downriver in their shantyboat.

Reverend George Cleaton Wilding was a Methodist circuit rider during the late 1800s and early 1900s who traveled the mountains of West Virginia preaching. When he was about ten years old, around 1856, he lived in New Haven and worked as an errand boy for a store in Hartford. George often heard of the story of a haunting on Sliding Hill. But even at a tender age, he scoffed at the idea of ghosts. Back in those days, there was only a raggedy bridle path between New Haven and Hartford, and one day, still in the early hours of the morning, George was hurrying to work on this trail. Before him, he saw a colonial officer approaching him on horseback.

The boy stopped and stared, mesmerized, admiring the mighty horse and the grand uniform the rider wore, complete with a shiny sword at his belt. As the rider neared to less than 25 steps between the two and by a small creek of water trickling across the path, young George looked down long enough to jump across as not to get his shoes wet. When he looked up again, the rider had mysteriously vanished. So struck by the strange occurrence, the boy followed the trail to Hartford and found no hoofprints or sign that the rider had even passed!

The ghosts that step forth from twilight to the still hours of the night are those bearing lanterns to search fruitlessly for a hidden treasure. As the story goes, early settlers traveling along the Ohio River camped below the hill for the night. Within their boat, they carried many gold coins to buy some land. Unknown to them, thieves aware of their cargo had followed them.

In the dark of night, while the party slept, the thieves came upon the boat and murdered the settlers. They stuffed the bodies within a ledge and hid the gold coins until they could return for them at a safer, later date when suspicious fingers would not point at them for the raiding. They let the boat float down the river.

Unfortunately for the murdering lot, they were all killed within the next year. However, on one thief's deathbed, he admitted to the murder and hiding the treasure. Not long after, the mysterious lights would begin. Later, many would search for the coins, but nobody found them. One by one, those who sought out the treasure were struck dead by some foul means and were cursed to come back in a ghostly form to search out the gold for eternity.

Meigs County

Buffington Island Battlefield Memorial Park
56890 Ohio River Scenic Byway
Portland, Ohio 45770
39.002455, -81.773959

Ghost Soldiers of Buffington Island Battlefield

Ghostly soldiers have been seen at this Civil War battlefield.

On July 19th, 1863, while trying to cross the rising waters of the Ohio River near a ford called Buffington Island after a Civil War raid into Ohio, Confederate Calvary leader John Morgan and over 2400 of his men were attacked on a flood plain just outside of Portland. An estimated 52-120 Confederate soldiers and 25 Union soldiers were killed on the battlefield. There have been sightings of soldiers seen atop horses and tiny dancing lights in the four acres of battlefield operated by the Ohio Historical Society.

Lawrence County

Woodland Cemetery
824 Lorain Street
Ironton, Ohio 45638
38.507274,-82.648602

Slapped Lady Grave

Of course, I had to try it! And yes, crazy as it sounds, it was warm!

Osa Wilson was the wife of a leading businessman in Ironton. She had been married nearly seventeen years and was also a mother of six when she became ill with colitis and neuritis. She died just one month later, in February of 1911, at the age of 33. Osa's burial was in the Woodland Cemetery, and legends follow the statue of a tumultuous marriage, a pregnancy, and a flight down a staircase by hands unknown. The figure has a handprint donning the left cheek, a sinister slap from her killer. If you press your palm to her belly, there is a certain warmth emanating from the stone.

Washington County

Anchorage House
(aka Putnam Villa/Douglas Putnam House)
498 George Street
Marietta, Ohio 45750
39.413551, -81.463473

Floating Eliza

The Putnam in its heyday. Before the ghosts.

In the 1850s, it took ten years for Douglas Putnam to build this home for his wife, Eliza. It cost an extravagant $65,000, but Eliza had to have it. Eliza fell in love with a friend's home during a visit to New Jersey, and it became the model for her own house in Marietta. It has twenty-two rooms and a tower room with a widow's walk. The Italian villa has sandstone walls quarried from neighboring hills and overlooks the city of Marietta and both the Ohio and Muskingum Rivers. It was initially called 'Putnam Place,' and not until it changed hands later, was it renamed 'The Anchorage House.'

It hosted many functions for the well-to-do of Marietta. Eliza passed away in September of 1862 from heart disease, only three years after the initial construction of the home. She was 53-years-old. It remained in the family until a couple of years after Douglas died, and his third wife sold it to the Harry Knox family, owners of Knox Boatyard. They renamed it the Anchorage. The Anchorage changed hands several times before it became a nursing home for about fifty patients in 1960 and renamed The Christian Anchorage. By 1984, all the patients had moved to the more modern Marie Antoinette Pavilion right next door.

When it was a nursing home, patients, nurses, and aides would see a shadowy woman on the stairs near the dining room. One nurse also reported seeing a woman in period clothing walking from the stairway to the dining area. And on another occasion, an aide also saw a phantom light wiggling its way across the widow's walk on top. Eliza's ghost has been seen both inside the home and outside.

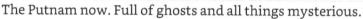

The Putnam now. Full of ghosts and all things mysterious.

While hiking one afternoon in Zaleski, I came upon a couple who visited the home one afternoon and were more than happy to tell me their story of the Anchorage House. The pair told me that after pulling into the graveled side road to the Anchorage, they got out of their cars. Just as the woman turned to head toward the building, she stopped. Not a stone's throw away was a full-bodied apparition of a woman floating several feet above the grassy lawn!

The Washington County Historical Society now owns the property. Hidden Marietta guides and paranormal investigators provide haunted history tours. Today, Eliza pops up once in a while to surprise those visiting this historic site. You may see her shadow while she peers out of one of the windows or walking the hallways and stairways. Spectral voices resonate in the building, and shadow figures prowl the many rooms. Those who have attended ghostly tours have had their hair tugged and touched. And if you are lucky (or unlucky depending upon your views of ghostly surprises), you might see a spooky dead woman floating around the yard!

Monroe County

Monroe Lake
OH-800
Jerusalem, Ohio 43747
39.819517, -81.136092

Do Not Look Down—Peer into the Dark Depths and THEY Will Peer Back

I went here on a cool day in March and tried my luck with the legend. The lake had a beautifully haunting feel to it along with herons and kingfishers flying around.

If you gaze into the water of Monroe Lake, faces will peer back at you from the murky depths of their watery grave. They are those who have drowned in the meandering Baker Fork feeding into Monroe Lake over the years when it flooded. Now they are stuck in its calm dammed waters, unable to move on.

Gallia County

Gallipolis Island
Clendenin, West Virginia 25515
38.813992, -82.192220
Stewart Road Below Mooney Cemetery
1936 Stewart Road
Crown City, Ohio 45623

A Creepy Island and a Road

Gallipolis Island.

Gallipolis Island, along the Ohio River, was found in 1770 along with its much-coveted wild grapes used to produce wine. It would become a resort in the 1840s with a beach and picnic area, and in the 1860s, steamboats were built on the island. The West Virginia Land Trust now owns it. It is not without its share of the otherworldly fare. Passing through so many hands, it is not surprising it has a few ghosts in its midst. Spectral lights bob on the island, spotted by those driving past in their cars.

Mooney Cemetery is nearly lost to time on a hill in Gallia County. When driving their carriages along Stewart Road beneath it in earlier days, folks heard the low music of a fiddle playing softly while Matthew Mooney soothed his dead daughter, 5-year-old Elizabeth, who passed in 1854, with song.

Stewart Road by Mooney Cemetery.

Jackson County

Salem Church Cemetery
Route 124 and Salem Road
Wellston, Ohio 45692
39.078658, -82.501895

Knock-Knock Ghost

Salem Church—knock-knock and it might knock-knock back.

The Salem Cemetery is the site of the monument honoring the unknown Confederates killed during a Civil War battle nearby when General John Morgan made his infamous raid through Ohio in July of 1863. Several of Morgan's men were killed when they crossed paths with Ohio militia on the hillsides of nearby Berlin Crossroads. Between 4 and 12 were killed, have been buried nearby, and may haunt the cemetery. The church is home to the Knock-Knock Ghost. If you knock-knock gently on the door, you may hear someone—or *something* knock-knock back.

Muskingum County

Stumpy Hollow
10245 Norwich Drive
Norwich, Ohio 43767
39.982859, -81.796340

Stumpy

Stumpy Hollow

In the early 1800s, the Federal Government built the National Road connecting the eastern and western states. In Ohio, along the route were the larger towns of Cambridge and Zanesville, and about halfway between the two was the smaller village of Norwich—each providing stagecoach stops along the road. It is near Norwich, where downhill winding curves made for more than a few harrowing experiences for stagecoach drivers.

One encounter was in August of 1835. Thirty-five-year-old Christopher Baldwin, who was a librarian of the American Antiquarian Society, was traveling by stagecoach to research ancient burial mounds around southern Ohio. As the carriage driver sped through the turns, a farmer with a drove of hogs swept out into the street. The pigs spooked the horses, the stagecoach overturned, and Baldwin died.

A few years would pass after the incident, and during the 1840s, the village doctor was visiting a sick patient around midnight. His travels took him down the main street of Norwich, just past the cemetery, and then along a path that leads through a dark hollow. It was here that he heard rustling sounds in the brush and credited it to deer moving in to rest for the night. He had made these nightly treks often, and the town was safe—he felt no fear. That is until something strange barreled upward from the far end of the hollow, rushing straight at him.

The doctor towed on the reins, and his horse stumbled backward, but not before the man took in the terrifying sight—a ghostly figure atop a horse and it had no head, just a stumpy knob at the end of his neck! Then the headless horseman disappeared. The doctor's horse reared, almost tossing him from his saddle before bolting back to town. The doctor told his story to neighbors and they laughed, one even deciding to disprove him. At midnight, the skeptic went into the hollow on foot. He, too, found himself face to face with the headless rider.

This ghostly figure would show in many forms, some even describing it as a man-faced dog. But all knew whose ghost it was—nicknamed Stumpy for the stubby knob of the headless neck. It was that of Christopher Baldwin—a spirit stuck on earth and never able to get to his destination to finish his work and who rode from his place of death to the cemetery where he was buried.

Morgan County

Brick Church Cemetery and Historical Marker
1790 OH-376
Stockport, Ohio 43787
39.568537, -81.780252

No Dancing on the Grave, Babe

The grave of Captain Isaac Hook and a legend.

The first known burial at Brick Church Cemetery was in 1829, and it is still active. It is also where Captain Isaac Newton Hook is buried next to the river with a unique grave. Captain Hook was a well-known businessman in Morgan County. He owned a general store in the mid-1840s and was also the captain of two steamboats on the Muskingum River. Folks always talked that he did not get along with his second wife. When he passed on, he had an unusual tomb made with a rounded top, 'so his wife could not dance on top of his grave when he died.'

Noble County

Shenandoah Crash Site
50526-50528 OH-821
Ava, Ohio 43711
39.830643, -81.574108

Unearthly Shadows Over the Sky

The USS Shenandoah

It was September 3rd, 1925, when the dirigible USS Shenandoah, on a publicity tour, came crashing to the earth during a storm. The crash site was in three different locations, with the stern section falling at Ava in Noble County, and fourteen crew members died. Travelers through the area have reported a strange shadow hovering in the sky, a ghostly reminder of the Shenandoah's final flight. If you are driving along I-77 near Ava, keep an eye on the sky for the ghostly airship.

Guernsey County

Deep Cut on Route 40
14159-14015 US-40
Cambridge, Ohio 43725
40.036662, -81.478576

The Headless Ghost of Deep Cut

Working on the roadways, shoveling the small stones to make an easy path for travelers' wagons—and places for murderers to bury their victims.

In the early 1800s, the government built a road from the center of the United States westward, which could become a primary path for settlers. Called the National Road, it would later be known as Route 40. One employee working in the early years on the National Road frugally saved every cent he could and stashed it in his pockets. It was noted by several unscrupulous coworkers who followed him one night along the new road.

They murdered him in cold blood for his money, cutting off his head so no one would recognize the man. They shoveled the small stones used to cover the road over his body near a deep cut in a hill they had recently completed. The killers buried his head elsewhere. Since the death, the murdered man can be seen in supernatural form, headless and stumbling along Route 40 between Old Washington and Cambridge at what locals call The Deep Cut, searching for his head.

Deep Cut on the Old National Road where a ghost stumbles around looking for his head.

Belmont County

Louiza Catherine Fox Murder Site
Twp Hwy 546 B (Starkey Road)
Barnesville, Ohio 43713
40.104476,-81.174702

Two Ghosts. One Monster.

The site of the Louiza Fox murder and where ghosts are seen.

On a bare hillside of old strip-mined land at Egypt Valley Wildlife Area, a lone stone with an inscription sits. It marks the murder place of Louiza Fox. And some have seen her ghost silently pacing there. Here is her story—

Thirteen-year-old Louiza Fox was returning to her family farm near Sewellsville on a late afternoon in January 1869. The pretty young girl was a live-in housemaid for the Hunter family, a local coal mine owner.

One of the miners in Hunter's employ, 22-year-old Thomas Carr, had been pursuing the little girl relentlessly since the previous autumn. He had, several times, accompanied her from work to home. John Fox, Louiza's father, questioned Carr with a wary eye, but the miner insisted he only walked with Louiza to watch over her because of her tender age. Louiza refused any idea of courting the older man again and again. Finally, however, it was brought to her father's attention by Louiza herself that Carr had asked her to marry him some weeks later. The child begged her father to refuse the peculiar, threatening, and unpleasant man; she had no interest in him.

When Carr confronted the father to ask her hand in marriage, John Fox kindly excused the askance, telling Carr that Louiza was too young. Perhaps in maybe two or three years if he proved himself worthy by keeping a job and purchased a bit of land AND if the young woman, who would be closer to marriageable age, was willing, he could ask for her hand again. But during the last weeks of January, knowing her brief time working at the Hunter family's home was coming to an end, Carr's menacing presence had increased. Although Louiza and her father both thwarted continued advances and gift-bestowing by Carr, his stalking had come to a head on that fateful day as he followed her from room to room, asking her to marry him.

Noting Carr's strange behavior, Louiza's employer tried to persuade the young girl to stay at the Hunter house for her safety until they could take her home by horseback. Louiza politely refused. Her home and other family members' homes were close by and just off what is now Starkey Road and near the Egypt Valley Wildlife Area. Besides, nobody in the tiny tight-knit community, not even Louiza, thought him dangerous. He was just another seasonal worker offering meager working and social skills.

Carr had already begun to believe the polite rebuttal offered by her father was just a formality in asking for her hand in marriage. In his irrational state, the odd miner thought that the well-mannered rebuffs from the sweet little girl were only to please her father, and she was simply hiding whatever love or lust she felt for him behind her modesty. It was, in fact, her 6-year-old brother, Willy, sent to escort her home when worried about her welfare returning from the Hunter home. Carr had demanded for the last time to speak with John Fox and had threatened the man to give his daughter's hand to him in marriage—or else. John refused him.

After Willy and Louiza began to walk home, Carr waylaid the two on the path. She tried desperately to allude him along the isolated roadway by running and hiding at some points. Then as Louiza and her little brother passed a small chestnut orchard a stone's throw from home, Carr made his move and crept from beside a fence by the trees and into their path. After sending the younger brother on his way, Carr asked the girl to marry him once again. She refused, telling him that she was far too young to be wed.

Carr then pulled a razor from his pocket, and tossed her by one shoulder to the ground. She called out in sobbing screams for her papa, and Thomas Carr slit her throat. By the time her father had hastened to the spot, he had found young Louiza lying dead in a small ditch by the road where Carr had dragged her during the short struggle.

There is a stone in Belmont County tucked into the Egypt Valley Wildlife Area marking the place where Carr murdered Louiza. It is not the only sign Carr killed her there—her ghost walks the grassy hillside. She is silent because the razor to her throat spoilt any ghostly screams for help.

The ditch where Louiza's body was dragged. Above, the marker left as a memorial.

Carr was hunted down, found guilty of murder, and eventually hanged. They buried him in an unmarked grave at the Methodist Cemetery in St. Clairsville. Before death, he confessed to killing fourteen others, although some believed he fabricated most of those murders. But there was one confession many believed did hold some truth. Among those Carr acknowledged killing was another man—a German immigrant by the name of Alois Ulrich. Along with Joseph Eisele (also known as the Parkersburg Hatchet Slayer), he admitted to helping murder the man by bashing his head to a pulp with a stone in the Wheeling Tunnel in June of 1867 for the small amount of money in Ulrich's pocket. The body of Ulrich was dragged from the tunnel and concealed in a culvert.

After death, Ulrich was not silent. Not long after the murder in Wheeling Tunnel, the ghostly form of the murdered man began to appear emerging on the ceiling swathed in the green slime, indeed gathered from the dead patrons left in an old cemetery above the tunnel along with his own rotten flesh. His arm extended with bloody fingers hanging half-severed from the stems.

The forefinger of the other hand pointed desperately at his temple where a gash lay, fresh but with dark, clotted blood. With unmoving lips, those who ran into the ghost of Ulrich would hear his blood-curdling moans and listen to the fight ensue that left him dead before the guttural words came from his throat: "Let the dead rest!"

Hempfield Tunnel in Wheeling just over the Ohio line where another ghost from Carr's murdering hand may haunt.

You can visit the sites, and perhaps see at least two of the ghosts that one monster left behind. But be wary. Not far from the memorial for little Louiza, there was once a coal heap for the Fox's home. It is there that Thomas Carr would later creep up into the shadows before he was apprehended.

He hid behind the dump with a gun he had procured from a neighbor. The killer crouched there for hours, lurking, listening to the family mourn, waiting, watching, stalking the girl even after death. He returned there to collect Louiza and her soul to keep forever, like a ghoul returning to a grave to feast upon the remains.

His dark spirit is there even today. If you are not careful, he might not see the ghost of sweet Louiza who is said to pass by the grassy lawn and relive her horrid last moments struggling with Carr on the ground. Instead, it will be your soul the prowling Carr takes after he creeps up from hell. Then he will snatch you up and drag you back down with him and dine upon you —

The memorial for Louiza Fox at the murder site.

Louiza Fox Grave where she is also said to wander in ghostly form—Salem Cemetery Barnesville, Ohio (40.089460, -81.153695)

Louiza Fox Murder Site:
Twp Hwy 546 B
Barnesville, Ohio 43713
(40.104476,-81.174702)

Alois Ulrich Murder Site
Hempfield Tunnel on Wheeling
Heritage Trail
Wheeling, WV 26003
(40.073096, -80.711017)

Northwestern Ohio

Sandusky County

Bridge over Muddy Creek
2903 Fought Road
Lindsey, Ohio 43442
41.422921, -83.201654

Elmore Rider—Ghost Light

A ghostly motorcycle rider is seen near the towns of Lindsey and Elmore, the aftermath of a broken pledge of love. The story has been around for a while. The article below comes from the Cleveland Plain Dealer November 24th, 1922.

"GHOST LIGHT" SHINING

Port Clinton Mystery Renewed; Curious Go Miles to See It.

(Plain Dealer Special)

PORT CLINTON. O., Nov. 23.—The so-called "Ghost Light" which appears at night on the road between Lindsey and Oak Harbor, again is attracting the attention of Port Clinton residents. They are making trips to the spot where the light has been reported to have made its nocturnal appearance for many years. Atmospheric conditions, it is said, cause the light to be more brilliant at times.

Its mysterious appearance and disappearance have caused many to drive for miles to witness this spectacular illusion.

There is a ghost light about 30 miles from Toledo near the towns of Lindsey and Oak Harbor. Old legends relate a house was haunted by an old man who shot himself. He threatened beforehand to return after death.

A later story explains the lights with more romantic flair—it is about a couple who pledged their love to each other just as World War I broke out. The young man was sent off to war and fought overseas. The two wrote back and forth for a year, long letters of love and heartache, and missing each other, then the letters from the man simply stopped coming. Heartbroken, the young woman was sure her sweetheart was dead.

The bridge as it appeared in yesteryears. Courtesy of the Harris-Elmore Public Library, Grace Luebke Local History Collection.

On March 21st of 1918, he returned from the war. Why he had not written his sweetheart, is not told. But to surprise the young woman as he neared her home, he shut off his motorcycle along the roadway the evening of his return and snuck to her window and peered inside. The woman who pledged her life to him was with another man. Distraught, the young man sped off on his motorcycle, not heeding his speed, nor ruts in the old farm road. Suddenly, the bike hitched, and he tumbled off near a small bridge over Muddy Creek. He was decapitated by barbed fence wire running along the fields. Now, legends tell that on March 21st each year, the Elmore Rider returns. People see ghostly lights along Fought Road, where it crosses Muddy Creek.

Seneca County

Republic Train Tracks
Tracks near S Kilbourne Street
Republic, Ohio 44867
41.119210, -83.021740

Republic Ghost Train

Republic train tracks—a train rolls past the scene of a tragic accident in 1887 and where a ghostly train has been witnessed.

On a chilly January 4th of 1887 at 1:15 a.m., Lynn Fletcher, conductor, was heading east and leaving Tiffin in a freight train hauling 19 cars full of barrel hoops and staves. It was a single track, only allowing the use of one train at a time. He was aware a passenger train—the B & O Express Engine #726—was working its way westward on its passage from New York and would pass his train while it headed to Chicago. He also knew it should be an easy drive to the passing siding, a small spur in Republic where he could pull off and allow the much faster express train to pass safely.

However, the temperatures were falling fast and dropped to nearly ten degrees below zero. Fletcher's older, cumbersome freight train came upon an incline in the track and, due to the cold, began to lose steam. Realizing it was moving too slowly and the other train, moving at 60-miles-per-hour, was going to be coming before he could make the spur, Conductor Fletcher climbed up on the freight cars to flag the train to stop. It was sooner than expected that the conductor saw the passenger train rounding a bend. Desperately, he lifted his lantern in warning to the passenger train engineer, Lem Eastman. Eastman hit the brakes, but the two trains collided. Only the anguished cries of the passengers within the oncoming train filled the air along with the explosion of metal to metal.

The number of passengers killed may never be known, but estimates remain at 15 to 19 dead. People in the nearby village buried the unclaimed and unidentified (many burned beyond recognition) in the nearby Farewell Retreat Cemetery in Republic. But the story of the ill-fated train would not end there. Within just a few months, tiny lights began to show up along the tracks. And one evening, as the Express No 5 train approached the area of the wreck, the engineer saw a red light—a distress signal wagging in the air. He applied the brakes and reversed the engines, and the train came to a standstill on the exact spot of the train wreck. And yet, no one was there. The light disappeared. But just before the train came to a halt, both the engineer and the fireman swore they saw who carried the lantern—a woman wearing a filmy white dress. The apparition showed up to other engineers, and ghostly lights still appear where the train wreck occurred and all the way to the cemetery and location of the unknown graves.

Seneca County

Josiah Hedges Park
30 Park Place
Tiffin, Ohio 44883
41.113092, -83.172114

Eerie Blend of Old and New in Tiffin

Josiah Hedges Park—a pretty park with a ghastly past.

There is a little park in Tiffin with a swing set, picnic area, and plenty of room for children to let loose their energy. It is Josiah Hedges Park, where kids can play in the sunshine and perhaps get their toes wet wading in Rock Creek. Just remember, though, in August of 1834, a cholera epidemic broke out, leaving 63 dead in its wake with many buried at one of the old town cemeteries.

Over the years and as the town grew around it, most of the bodies were exhumed due to the erosion of Rock Creek nearby—not only were graves exposed, but some corpses were even swept away during flooding. Now that cemetery is Josiah Hedges Park. And those little giggles of children playing or the occasional moan you think is wind slipping through the trees might be an eerie blend of old and new, some leftover from the land's past.

Riverside Drive
Tiffin, Ohio 44883
(41.117141, -83.176690)

While you are in town—March 25th-26th, 1913 marked the date of the destructive flood that nearly devastated Tiffin as the Sandusky River overflowed its banks and killed nineteen people. Take a walk along the river, and you just might run into some of the ghosts swept away on that horrible day.

Fulton County

Goll Woods State Nature Preserve And Goll Cemetery
26000-26998 Township Hwy Ef
Stryker, Ohio 43557
41.556171, -84.367344

Calling Maryann

Most cemeteries are closed dusk to dawn. However, no worries—a little ghost girl wanders the woods night or day, so you may get a peek at her if you visit!

Goll Woods is 100 acres of land set aside from the 1837 settlement of Peter and Catherine Goll, French immigrants. A hundred acres of this land was left unspoiled and much like the Great Black Swamp area that once surrounded it. Goll Cemetery is within the bounds of the nature preserve of Goll Woods. If you stand in front of Maryann Goll's grave on a moonless night, you will awaken her spirit from its deathly slumber. A mist will rise, forming into Maryann before she travels slowly to nearby children's graves and weeps for their early deaths.

Lucas County

Martin Luther King Bridge
The Old Cherry Street Bridge
1 Main Street
Toledo, Ohio 43605
41.651094,-83.526147

Barefoot Ghost Dragging a Rope on the Old Cherry Street Bridge

Old Cherry Street Bridge

It is known as the Martin Luther King Bridge now. It spans the Maumee River in Toledo, connecting Cherry Street with Main. Long ago, when it was a different bridge and one with a toll to cross the river, it was known as the Cherry Street Bridge. Back then and when the city built the first Cherry Street Bridge in 1865, it was wood. It cost 2 cents a person to cross the bridge and a dime for a horse.

Between 1865 and 1883, the bridge would be wiped out by floods two times. Finally, in 1884, a new steel bridge was built lasting until 1908. It was safe from floods but not being hit by steamships. In 1908 a boat hit the Cherry Street Bridge, and a new concrete arch crossing was completed in 1914 to replace it.

Yet, if we take a step back in time to August of 1882 when the bridge was still made of wood and the new steel bridge of 1884 had yet to be built, a ghost appeared there. It was not just one time, but countless times over the years, for many people crossed over it to get to the central business district and a busy section of town. A local shoemaker named Joseph "Pop" Meyers had hanged himself there with a piece of rope, and soon after, so did his son—with the same rope. A Cincinnati Enquirer reporter interviewed Detective Louis Trotter of the Toledo Police Department in December of 1884. Trotter tells the story like this: *Some of the boys who live on the East Side were going home from duty one August morning in 1882. When we reached the first pier I was horrified to see the body of someone hanging there. It did not take us long to cut the corpse down and we found it was Pop Meyers, as he was familiarly called. His face was just as pleasant as if he were selling a pair of shoes to a customer. There was not the least sign of pain, and his wide-open eyes were looking rather expectantly up the river. He had evidently put on a new shirt, collar, and necktie, and was well dressed, except that he had no coat or shoes on. Well, we carried him home and found some letters which plainly indicated that his mind had left his body. His son, who had brought so much care on the old man's mind by his dissipation, begged us to give him the rope with which his father had hanged himself. 'I want it as a reminder,' he said, 'of my father.' Well, some way he obtained the rope, and with it, shortly afterward, ended his life at the identical spot, with the same rope.*

Soon after the deaths of the father and son, people began reporting a ghost on the bridge. The apparition was of a nicely dressed man dragging a rope. As he plodded across the bridge, no sound was made. His feet were bare just as the police officers had found him when he hanged himself. In fact, Trotter went on to state, *I investigated the affair and found it was true something was haunting the bridge. The ghost was dressed just as Meyers was on the morning that I cut him down. The old bridge was carried away, and the story was forgotten. The first night the new bridge was opened late wayfarers were badly frightened by a phantom walking slowly along in his bare feet, making no noise as he softly trod the planks. That's all I know about it. Officer Kruse states that many people have recently told him they had seen Meyers' ghost patrolling the bridge, rope in hand, after midnight.*

Cherry Street Bridge today.

Even after the new bridge was built in 1884, the ghostly apparition of Meyers was seen on the bridge. It does not seem to deter the old ghost that new bridges with new names have come after. There are still those who see a misty apparition walking along the Cherry Street Bridge when they cross over on foggy nights after midnight. And as long as people need to cross the Maumee, there probably always will!

Ottawa County

Johnson's Island
Confederate Stockade Cemetery
Marblehead, Ohio 43440
41.500592, -82.729641

Confederate Ghosts on Johnson's Island

Johnson's Island Cemetery and the monument—where ghostly soldiers rise from the grave to the tune of the statue's bugle.

Johnson's Island is a small island located in northern Ohio's Sandusky Bay. In 1861, the U.S. Army leased 40 acres of land belonging to the island's owner, Leonard Johnson, to build a camp for Confederate officer-rank prisoners-of-war during the U.S. Civil War. From 1862 to 1865, nearly 10,000 soldiers were housed at the prison camp, usually between 2000 to 3000 at a time. It had a hospital, barracks, kitchen, dining area, and cemetery for the prisoners. Disease and harsh winters took their toll on many of the soldiers; there are nearly 200 buried on the island.

The Island later became a resort in the late 1800s. In the early 1900s, miners quarried limestone there, and quarry owners built a village for the 150 or so men and their families which included a general store, school, tavern, and post office. The workers, who were mostly Italian, related many ghost stories over the years.

A 4758 The Stone Quarry, Johnsons Island, Sandusky, O.

Stone quarrying on Johnson's Island circa early 1910s. Stone quarry workers watched in wonder right here as ghosts appeared from the Confederate cemetery. *From the collection of: DSap's Postcards.*

Old legends tell that one stormy night in 1915, some of these Italian laborers working in the limestone and stone quarry on Johnson's Island saw the Confederate statue at the cemetery turn from where it faced the lake so that it was looking toward the graves behind it. Then, when it lifted its bugle high and blew a tune, ghostly soldiers in rotting Confederate uniforms slipped from the mist coming from the lake and marched away. Old-timers tell that quarry workers heard a constant humming of the song *Dixie*, echoing across the old camp.

Defiance County

Defiance County Children's Home Cemetery
Defiance, Ohio 43512
41.346149, -84.421203

Ghostly Giggles Burping Up from the Earth

All that remains of the old Defiance Children's Home open through mid-October 1914—a cemetery and little spooks.

The Defiance County Children's Home was in operation from 1884 to 1914. It sat on 22 acres and could accommodate about 40 children. The buildings are gone, the cemetery nearly lost to time except for a few sparse graves. But the spirit of the young orphans who lived there are still around. Visitors relate hearing soft children's whispers and giggles erupting from deep in the earth above the graves. Where the sounds arise, tiny dancing lights flit about and then vanish.

Paulding County

Paulding County Jail
112 S Williams Street
Paulding, Ohio 45879
41.136871, -84.581152

Unfinished Whodunit

The Paulding County Jail—The place for not-so-nice ghosts, obscure secrets, and an unfinished whodunit or two.

The old Paulding County Jail is haunted. Built in 1874, it stayed in use until 2006. Over the years, it has collected spirits in the same way kids collect eggs in an Easter basket—eagerly snatching up any it could find. More than a handful of ghosts reside here, and a few of those who died did so under strange circumstances.

Some are not so nice—they might push, tug hair, and scratch. But who could expect less? It was a jail. A few have also suggested the ghost of a teen lingers there. In the early 1960s, a fourteen-year-old girl named Nancy was walking home with her little sister from the movies in Paulding. As the girls strolled along the walkway, a car pulled up beside them. A man got out, grabbed Nancy, pulled her into the vehicle, and drove away. Only a few hours later, hunters found Nancy's corpse.

Years would pass, and police never found Nancy's killer. Evidence collected from her case was supposed to be kept in the jail, but it vanished. While renovating the building, hidden chambers were unearthed in the cellar. Deep within those chambers, someone discovered a part of a dress and a shoe. Nancy's mother identified them as belonging to her daughter. Not so strangely, then, it is believed this girl haunts the jail because her crime has yet to be solved, nor has her killer been brought to justice.

Mercer County

Crybaby Bridge
Palmer Road Crossing Over
St. Marys River
Mendon, Ohio 45862
40.680356, -84.561397

Crybaby Bridge and Glowing Grave of Palmer Road

Crazy stuff happens on Palmer Road. I always tell people not to stop in the middle of the road on crybaby bridges. Pull to the side. If a ghost wants to get you, it will find you both places.

A mother, father, and baby were picnicking beneath the bridge crossing the St. Mary's River when the devil showed up, snatched each by the collar, and dragged them all down to hell. If you pause above, he will take you too, but only if you hear the baby's cry.

Another legend for the bridge tells that a man murdered his family and dropped them into the river below. Then he hanged himself on a nearby tree. If you stop your car there, you will hear a baby's cries. Right after, a ghost will appear and walk straight through your car, and then it will not start. You have to push your vehicle to get it started again!

The cemetery to the rear of the gate has a glowing grave. Note the strange white anomaly just above the arch. It appears to be shooting from the old graveyard!

Down the same road about a half-mile, is Palmer Cemetery far back in a field. Privately owned, you have to view it from the roadway, and per the legend, you are supposed to be in the road anyway. At one time, two concrete lions perched on the archway entrance to the cemetery that is right along Palmer Road, guarding the old burying grounds (you can see the graveyard in the background, left). Their green glass eyes glowed against the moonlight spooking horses so often, they had to cover the statues with bags. You cannot see more than a portion of a lion's paw now, but you can check out the glowing grave at the cemetery far back in the field—it shows up at a certain angle while driving past.

Mercer County

Tomlinson Cemetery
12860-12998 Tomlinson Road
Rockford, Ohio 45882
40.727812, -84.550710

Disappearing Trick in a Cemetery

Tomlinson Cemetery along the Mercer-Van Wert line.

There is a wicked little trick you can do in a cemetery located on the Mercer-Van Wert county line. If one person stands in the middle of Tomlinson Cemetery and a second person walks backward around it, the person in the center vanishes. But where? I do not know. Nor do I know how to get them back, so do not ask.

And if you look across the street, you will see the location of Wesley Chapel before the empty building burned to the ground. The land held the first churches in the area, and people came 30 miles for meetings in the buildings. When the church was still there, rumors spread an altar boy haunted the interior. You could hear his footsteps within.

This was once the site of a big, beautiful church with a ghostly past—Wesley Chapel. (40.728055, -84.552210) until an arsonist burned it down around 2010. The ruins of this building are on *private* property. You can see it from the road, but please do not trespass!

A historical article about the church mentions that James Smith, a Sunday School superintendent, died in Sunday School at the church. Perhaps over the years, the story mutated, and it was the sound of his footsteps people heard within and not an altar boy.

Van Wert County

Co Hwy 103
Rockford, Ohio 45882
40.729899, -84.551794

County Line Ghost

This lonely road may not be so lonely. It has a ghost.

Just north of Tomlinson Cemetery, a pale, ghostly form flits in front of cars at the little wooded lots. With a church once located here, it was a busy place on Sunday mornings suggesting it is a long-dead parishioner waiting for services to begin again.

Van Wert County

Woodland Cemetery
10968 Woodland Avenue
Van Wert, Ohio 45891
40.867476, -84.617820

Dead Man Walking

An older, out-of-the-way section of the cemetery at Van Wert.

On a warm June evening in the 1880s, a Methodist minister visited relatives on Willshire Road in Van Wert. The time had passed quickly as he sipped lemonade on the front porch and chatted until the moon crept up and over the horizon. Then, as the crickets began to chirp, he realized the roads would be dark. He excused himself to leave, but those within the home advised against it. It was a two-hour walk to his house, robbers could be lurking about, and a strange and possibly malevolent shade was seen at Woodland Cemetery. Surely, he should stay for the night.

The minister had scoffed at his hosts' worries, waylaid their doubts with a shake of the head, and decided he was quite amused at their ploys to get him to stay longer. Ghosts of all things! He knew the cemetery well. It was only 10 to 12 years old, a larger piece of land had been cleared for newer burials while some older ones closer to town, exhumed and placed within its bounds. He knew no specter would be out rambling around the pretty little lot. Not only was it too modern, but there were no such things as ghosts.

A lonely stretch of road in front of Woodland Cemetery and a place a ghost would walk to his first place of rest.

The minister cheerfully bade them goodbye and went on his way, enjoying the warm evening walk. That is until he was just a few feet from the cemetery and caught sight of the headstones before him. He felt a horrible sense of loneliness then, almost suffocating as he took in the silhouette of evergreens making dark shadows lurking on the ground from the pale moon. Every childhood nightmare of ghosts chasing him through his dreams left the hairs standing up on the nape of his neck, his feet begging to walk faster. He could not pass that cemetery quickly enough!

Just as he was smack dab in the center, he watched as near a large, new headstone a tall, black cadaver arose from the soil clothed in a burial gown. The eyes were dark in its sockets, and what few teeth it owned clung to the dried hide peeling from its lips appearing like fangs. As the minister stood there frozen with mouth agape, the corpse turned its head in all directions, then set its eyes right on him, marching straight to where he stood.

The minister set off at a healthy pace toward town. Realizing the two would meet at the same point in the road, he slowed his steps, allowing the corpse to outdistance him, so it was about 20 feet ahead. The ghostly form kept a shuffling pace, oblivious now to the minister as he walked behind. Suddenly, it turned into a brushy area not far from the road. As the minister passed, trying to appear unconcerned, he noted he could not find the ghost even as he wagged his head frantically around. It had vanished entirely!

But then he saw something—a piece of the old burying ground, a secluded, neglected spot nearly lost in the scrubby grass, thickets, and weeds. The minister shuddered. It all came to light. The graveyard was the ghost's first resting place and should have been the last; however, well-meaning citizens moved the corpse to the newer Woodland Cemetery. And the dead man was having none of that!

Shelby County

Place of the Old Lockington Bridge
*11999-11691 Co Hwy 132
(Lockington-Kirkwood Road)
Piqua, Ohio 45356
40.209870, -84.214972*

Ghost of an Old Crybaby Covered Bridge

Left: Crybaby Bridge 1983 before an arsonist burned it down. *Image: Christdt*

Below: Crybaby Bridge today, where a concrete bridge now stands and perhaps still, a ghost.

For over 138 years, the Lockington Covered Bridge spanned the Miami River until it burned down in 1989. Now only its ghost remains—what is left is a modern concrete bridge where it used to rest. At one time, this was one of Northeastern Ohio's crybaby bridges. Although its story is lost to time, perhaps whatever ghost lurks there is not. One report I found centers around teens driving across the bridge and *something* BIG jumped on the roof of their car! They did not return to see what that *something* could have been.

Shelby County

Shelby County Historical Society
201 N Main Avenue
Sidney, Ohio 45365
40.287072, -84.155446

Old Funeral Home Spooks

The Shelby County Historical Society is worth a visit—and not just for the ghosts!

The Shelby County Historical Society building was the home of William Haslup, a partner in the lucrative Sidney Steel Scraper Company, until he died in 1912. The two-story house would later become a funeral home from the 1930s to 1999. With its long life as a funeral home, it has some ghostly activity, albeit mischievous. Staff report hearing the sound of chairs dragged across floors, and upon checking, nothing is amiss, and no furniture moved.

One worker made a quick dash into the historical society building at the end of a Christmas parade to drop off some baskets. She hastily placed them away, then made her way to the entrance, closing the door to the empty building before locking it tightly. As soon as she turned the key, the lights went on—and the only way to turn the lights off or on is within the building! It was no relief to her when she got to her car and realized that she had left her purse inside the building and had to return to fetch it.

It is not as if those working and volunteering there are gullible enough to think every knock and bang are ghosts. When the scraping sound of long fingernails on the metal blinds caught one worker's attention, she investigated to find it was the old water heater. But not all experiences can be explained. Take, for example, the little girl giggles heard in the upstairs rooms when no children are around, or the bag of pillowcases dropped off by a volunteer that mysteriously disappeared and could not be found even after a thorough search of every closet and cubbyhole in the old home. The pillowcases curiously appeared in the middle of the kitchen floor around Christmas.

If you visit (and you certainly need to visit for their seasonal ghost tours), you may get an overwhelming feeling that you simply MUST leave the building—and fast. Some have. Or you might hear screaming only to find out that no living person in the building cried out. You may listen to knocks and bangs and other sounds you cannot explain. But best of all, you will get to visit a building with a unique historical past—oh, and maybe meet some ghosts!

Allen County

Lima State Hospital Cemetery
394-398 E Chapman Road
Lima, Ohio 45801
40.773668,-84.094788

A Killer Walks in Lima State Hospital Cemetery

Celia's grave.

Celia Rose, a woman who murdered her family with Rough on Rats poison, was sent to the Lima State Hospital. She died in March of 1934. There is one white cross marking her grave at the cemetery. It blends into 475 others just like it. There are a couple of things different, though, about her grave. Celia's picture is on a worn wooden frame. And her spirit wanders nearby, shuffling around her burial place. For those who see Celia, she seems oblivious that they are there. Perhaps she is. Or scarier is the thought that maybe Celia Rose is quite aware of their presence, and something about them reminds the dead murderer of her family.

Hardin County

Ridgeway Cemetery
20569 Township Road 179
Ridgeway, Ohio 43345
40.524663,-83.553497

Touching Anna Bell's Grave

Anna Bell Davis's grave. Will you follow her to death? Notice the Yucca or Eternity Plant—they were planted to ward off evil, keep the dead from rising—or simply out of mourning.

We know little of Anna Bell Davis's life. She was born in 1862 and lived with her widowed mother, Nancy, and younger sister, Mary, at Bokes Creek. On October 15th, 1881, and at the tender age of 19, she died. The writing on her headstone reads: *Remember youth as you pass by, As you are now, so once was I. As I am now, so you must be, Prepare for death and follow me.* It is this eerie epitaph that draws people to her grave like an incantation summoning the living to their death. Her gravestone is said to feel warm to the touch.

Auglaize County

Bloody Bridge
County Highway 182
St Marys, Ohio 45885
40.617862,-84.352863

The Bloody Bridge

The Bloody Bridge along the towpath trail has a ghostly tale from the canal boat years.

From the 1840s to the 1860s, the Miami and Erie Canal was an essential mode of transportation in Ohio, running a good three hundred miles from Toledo to Cincinnati. Towns between included Maumee and Napoleon in the northern part of the state and Sharonville and Lockland to the south. Around the small towns of Spencerville and St. Marys, two boats—the Daisy and the Minnie Warren—would pass each other. Onboard the Minnie Warren was the captain's daughter, whose name christened the craft. She also cooked for those on board, riding faithfully with her father along the route.

Men, called drivers, led the canal boats and guided the mules pulling the vessels along the worn towpath beside the water. Jack Billings was a big, softhearted man and a driver for the Daisy. A moody man by the name of William Jones led the mules for the Minnie Warren. Both men fell in love with Minnie, but she only had eyes for Jack. When the boats passed, playful flirting by Minnie with Jack became an object of rivalry between the two men.

It was 1854 when William's jealousy peaked after a social event both Minnie and Jack attended. Late in the evening, as they walked home to the canal, they paused at the bridge. William was waiting for them in the shadows with an ax. In one stroke, he cut Jack down. Minnie was so terrified that she fell backward over the edge of the bridge and into the water below. Those who lived nearby heard the screams. They tried to rescue Minnie, but she drowned in the murky waters of the canal.

They found her body, laying it next to the bloody one of her sweetheart. Gone, they were. But each of the young lovers left their mark on the region. For forty years after they removed Jack's corpse from the bridge, the bloodstains soaked into the wood from his body remained. And hence, it received its name—Bloody Bridge. Those who looked over the edge of the bridge where Minnie died said they would see her face staring up at them from beneath the muddy canal water.

William Jones fled the scene of the carnage, disappearing into the chilly night. There was no trace of the man until years later when skeletal remains were found deep in an old well not far from Bloody Bridge. The talk around town was that the corpse was William Jones, who shot himself in misery over Minnie's death while he sat on the side of the well. But what nobody said aloud was what they truly believed—it was, most likely, vigilante justice.

Logan County

Harrod Cemetery and Highway 56
4900 Township Highway 56
Bellefontaine, Ohio 43311
40.423173, -83.782884

Beware the Hatchet Man

Beware the Hatchet Man on this road. And when you pass Harrod Cemetery, watch for his unmarked grave that glows bright green.

Andrew Hellman was a tailor by trade, arriving in America from Germany in 1817. To most with whom he crossed paths, he was well-mannered, good-looking, and had many friends. He married Mary Abel— blithe, buxom, and light-hearted, and within a short amount of time, he had built up a business and a farm on Township Highway 56 outside Huntsville. The couple had three children—two boys and a girl. One April morning of 1839, after his children had grown, Louisa (age 17), Henry (age 16), and John (age 12), awakened quite ill. Within a day, Louisa and John both died and were buried together in a grave.

At some point after her children's deaths, Mary recalled picking up a jug of milk, and upon seeing a powdery substance on it, she decided not to drink the liquid. It occurred to her someone may have poisoned her children. She kept the idea to herself, only once mentioning her fears to a sister in a note. It was, perhaps, too horrendous a thought the children's father would kill them. Or maybe it was fear. Unbeknownst to all around them, Mary and the children had been suffering horribly at Andrew's hand.

The next month, Mary sent her only surviving son, Henry, to live with her brother, George. Several days would pass, and no one heard from Mary. Finally, George's wife went to check on her and found Andrew Hellman alive and lying on the bed covered in blood and Mary's mutilated body lying on the floor, an ax slicing through her skull.

Andrew was questioned and jailed, but he fled to Maryland, changed his name to Adam Horn, and started anew with a farm. Then he married a young girl of only 16-years-old named Malinda. On a stormy, snowy night in March 1843, Andrew Hellman murdered his second wife in cold blood. He dismembered her body and hid the parts throughout the farm in old coffee bags and a trunk. This time, when arrested for the murder, Andrew was convicted and executed for his crimes. He also was given the name of Hatchet Man by those who heard his story. Nearly a thousand spectators came to watch him hang. But just about as many have probably driven along Township Highway 56 looking for his ghost. Some nights, his spirit runs along the street, a hatchet in his hand, waiting for some unknowing Samaritan to stop and give him a ride.

Putnam County

Blanchard Cholera Cemetery
State Route 224, Road 5F
Blanchard, Ohio 45856
41.023039,-83.923802

Voices at the Old Cholera Cemetery

Blanchard Cholera Cemetery.

Most of the burials in this little cemetery were made during the cholera outbreak in 1852. When the epidemic struck, families laid to rest many victims without markers and quickly as not to spread disease. Little marks the cemetery but a few raggedy gravestones, and sometimes, the ghostly sing-song voices of children wafting through the air and mixing eerily with the chatter of corn stalks from the surrounding fields blowing in the wind.

Williams County

Buck Cemetery
Williams Defiance County Line Rd
Stryker, Ohio 43557
41.42720, -84.42500

The Guardian

A ghostly light weaves along the trail to the cemetery.

A light wobbles and weaves along the tree-lined trail to the cemetery just ahead of visitors. The ghostly shadow of the Buck family forefather guards the headstones there, insisting those who tread farther to do so lightly.

Wyandot County

Colonel Crawford Burn Site Monument
Township Highway 300
Carey, Ohio 43316
40.923442, -83.328799

Circle of Fire at William Crawford's Grave

William Crawford's marker.

Along an isolated bank of the Tymochtee Creek and near an old cemetery in Northwestern Wyandot County, an apparition hovers enveloped in fire. It has been seen as early as the 1800s by settlers in the area. Old-timers explained the ghost like this—

William Crawford was a soldier in the French and Indian War and the American Revolutionary War. In 1782 and toward the end of the Revolutionary War, he led about 500 volunteers against Indian villages along the Sandusky River, hoping to surprise them. Unfortunately for Crawford, word had spread of his attack, and tempers were high. In March of the same year, American militia had cruelly massacred 96 peaceful Delaware at a missionary village in Gnadenhutten.

In June, just south of where the town of Carey now stands, the Indians, along with their British allies, met and captured Crawford's troops. Shortly after this defeat, Indians learned Crawford's men had been a part of the Gnadenhutten massacre. As a result, Indians brutally tortured Crawford along Tymochtee Creek and burned him at the stake.

Although no one knows the exact spot of the burning of Crawford, old accounts and old maps suggest it was at a point called High Bank along the Tymochtee Creek near the old Buell farm, which is on private property now. However, Ron Marvin, with the Wyandot County Historical Society, has researched in great depth the history behind the Crawford killing. He reveals that perhaps the actual site is, in reality, closer than once believed to the monument dedicated to William Crawford in the Ritchy cemetery and near the creek shore.

Wood County

Holcomb Road
Pemberville, Ohio 43450
41.340769, -83.484578

The Legend of Holcomb Woods

Holcomb Road—the place of legends, ghosts, and dead children.

There is a legend not far from Bowling Green. A school bus driver was taking a full load of children home for the day, and the route took them through a thickly-treed area along Holcomb Road. Suddenly the bus veered off the pavement and smashed into a tree. The driver perished instantly, the bus exploded, and all within died a fiery death. If you drive along the road, you can see the bus driver's face on the tree that was the scene of the bus crash. Two ghostly headlights will rush toward you from the far end of the road with the sound of children screaming, vanishing at the tree.

Hancock County

Weidler's Pass Railroad
6566 County Road 236
Findlay, Ohio 45840
41.073000, -83.593211

Headless Ghost of Weidler's Pass

Weidler's Pass—where a ghostly lantern weaves and bobs and a headless man walks the tracks.

The small section of tracks that once ran across B. Weidler's property had a short bypass lane to facilitate traffic. It was a passing siding or section of track paralleling the mainline and joined at both ends. An entire train could pull over at this section so another could pass in the opposite direction.

During a routine run in the chilly days of November of 1889, a freight train conductor named Jimmy Welsh was on this section of railway. Just past the roadway intersection, he plummeted from a car that had broken away from another. He tumbled to the tracks at a dizzying speed. Within seconds, the wheels of the train that had split into two sections crushed him. He was instantly beheaded.

A few short months later, trains running the Lake Erie and Western Railroad between Findlay and Fostoria began seeing a headless apparition carrying a lantern on their midnight run. As the lantern light danced about above the train tracks, it was clear that the ghost was searching for something along the ground in the exact spot that the conductor lost his head.

Henry County

Buckland Lock at the Wabash and Erie Canal
Old US-24
Liberty Center, Ohio 43532
41.419817, -83.900076

Lock Keeper Spook

Buckland Lock —haunted by an old lock keeper.

Ohio once had a series of locks along the Miami and Erie Canal system by the Maumee River near Grand Rapids at a now-defunct canal boomtown called Providence. One section where boats could come in along the slack waters of Providence Dam of the river was a guard lock called Buckland's Lock. Here, boats from the Gilead Canal across the Maumee River could lock into the Miami and Erie Canal. Then they could work through a series of locks, including Lock 44.

During the 1800s, as canal boatmen neared the Buckland Lock, they would hear cries and groans along the shoreline as if someone was in great pain. Louder, it would get until a mist would rise from the canal waters before their boat. Then the fog would form into the distinct, gaunt figure of a little old man. He would fumble around the sluice gates before stepping back and opening them wide. The boats would begin to pass through the lock only to find the gate closed. This strange occurrence would happen at each of the series of locks running this section of the canal, the old misty ghost reappearing and disappearing at each gate.

Locals used to explain the strange phenomenon like this:

The previous keeper of the locks at Providence during the 1880s was a heavy-drinking man named Bill Bellington. Near midnight after drinking heavily all day, there was a cry of alarm that Bellington's quarters were on fire. The next morning, locals discovered his charred body within his shack. Many believed that someone murdered him for money he had hidden within his home. For years after his death, the little old man continued to work the locks; his ghost appeared to boatmen and others along the canal at Buckland's Lock and Lock 44.

Northeastern Ohio

Lake County

Willoughby Village Cemetery
Willoughby, Ohio 44094
41.63931, -81.41083

Willoughby's Mysterious Girl in Blue

The mysterious girl in blue showed up in Willoughby two days before Christmas and died without a name on her grave—until—

She came into Willoughby on the last streetcar from Cleveland on the 23rd of December of 1933. She was let out of the car at Kirtland for lack of money to pay the fare. A kind gentleman stopped her and inquired if she needed assistance. When she asked where she could find a room for the night, he walked with her to Mary Judd's boarding house on 3rd Street in Willoughby. He helped her make arrangements to stay.

After settling in about eight in the evening, she retired to her room. The next morning, Christmas Eve, she asked Missus Judd (who described the girl as quiet and wistful) how she could get to the train station to inquire about a ticket and where she could attend church. Missus Judd gave her directions for both, and off the girl went—in the wrong direction. Laughing, Missus Judd chased the girl down and waved her the right way. It would not be long before the young woman returned and, after wishing the older woman a Merry Christmas, clutched her purse and prepared to leave once again.

From the boarding house, the girl left along the street, eventually leading her past the cemetery. Then, she worked her way along 2nd Street toward the New York Central Railroad tracks. From there, she disappeared behind a grove of maple trees, possibly looking for a shortcut across the rows of train tracks to get to the other side. With sudden urgency, she made a swift dart forward as if the young woman realized too late that the train was coming. It was too late. The eastbound train heading to New York burst past, giving her a sidelong blow that pitched her body along the side of the tracks.

She ducked behind some maples and made a dart toward these very tracks, not realizing there was an oncoming train.

She died instantly from a fractured skull. When local authorities recovered the body, they found little on her person but ninety cents, a brush, some pencils, and blank envelopes—and, some say, a ticket to Corry, Pennsylvania. Yet there was nothing inside to show who she was or the direction from which she had come. They carried her body to the local funeral parlor owned by James McMahon. The identification of the body was this: *She was five feet and four inches, weighed approximately 135 pounds, had red-brown hair and hazel eyes. She had high cheekbones. She was wearing a blue woolen dress and a blue wool coat, floral scarf, and blue shoes.* As her identity was a mystery and her clothing was blue, locals dubbed her Girl in Blue.

After several days and the young woman's body was not claimed, authorities buried her in the Willoughby Village Cemetery in a bare plot within a simple casket. No headstone marked the life or death of the young woman who had passed so softly and ephemerally through the town of Willoughby. However, the mystery of her identity piqued the curiosity of those in the community and across the United States. Some with missing daughters sent letters to the city officials asking if she was their child.

Several people stepped forward, maintaining they recognized this Girl in Blue. In April of 1934, police believed the mystery was solved when two little sisters in a West Virginia orphanage saw pictures of the deceased and identified her as their 20-year-old sister, Mary Dalbaugh. However, Mary quickly contacted an aunt to show she was alive and well and working in Cumberland, Maryland. Then, in May of 1934, a Mansfield resident named Budd Goodwin, misidentified the mysterious girl's effects as belonging to his missing wife, Elsie. Soon after, he received a call from his wife and a handwritten letter stating the body was not hers.

But the girl was not forgotten. In April of 1936, Hank Heaverly, the cemetery sexton, had collected enough funds to provide a marker for the young woman with a discounted rate from a tombstone dealer. There was enough money left to buy flowers for the grave. The headstone would state: *IN MEMORY OF THE GIRL IN BLUE/ KILLED BY TRAIN/ DECEMBER 24, 1933/ "Unknown but not forgotten."*

Within a month of funding the headstone and in May of 1936, the Sandusky Register reported that someone had solved the mystery of the Girl in Blue. Leo Klimczak, of suburban South Branch in Pennsylvania, was shown pictures of the mystery woman and identified her as his 21-year-old sister, Josephine, whose nickname was Sophie. She was the daughter of Polish immigrants Jacob and Kathryn Klimczak and had left her family's farm in Corry, Pennsylvania, along with her brother, and headed to Detroit.

Like many young people during the Great Depression, the two sought out jobs to help the family financially. However, neither could find work. Discouraged, they decided they had no choice but to abandon their search.

They were barely able to scrape up enough money for return fare home for Sophie. And that is how she ended up heading in that direction and Willoughby nearly penniless and lost, trying to find her way home.

Sophie's ghost is lingering near her grave. You can visit it. It is in the Willoughby Village Cemetery. If you enter from the Sharpe Avenue entrance, drive past the first intersecting road and three trees. It will be on the left— tenderly cared for and tucked under a Mulberry tree along with another stone marking the grave in front of the old— *Girl in Blue. Identified as Josephine Klimczak. The 24th of December, 1933.*

Erie County

Milan Cemetery
74-98 Broad Street
Milan, Ohio 44846
41.29333,-82.598654
Grave: 41.293652,-82.596503

Knock-Knock on Abbots Tomb

Abbot's Tomb—knock if you dare!

Within the Milan Cemetery, an old mausoleum sits next to a dried-up pond. The tomb belongs to the family of Ben and Lorena Abbot. It has a legend tied with it. The mausoleum faces the opposite direction than the other graves, so townsfolk thought that the Abbots did not want to be bothered after death. Most left them alone. But, some people like to pester others and would dare their friends to knock on the door. When they did, the indignant ghosts of Ben and Lorena would yell at them and bang back. Although they have moved the bodies of Ben and Lorena, a couple of other family members remain inside.

Cuyahoga County

Erie Street Cemetery
2254 East 9th Street
Cleveland, Ohio 44115
41.497039,-81.683654

Joc-O-Sot

Erie Street Cemetery is the final resting place for settlers and two American Indians. One haunts the grounds—Joc-O-Sot, chief of the Sauk. Although he fought against the U.S. in the Black Hawk War, he later became a fishing guide along the lakeshore. Joc-O-Sot died in 1844 at age 34 and wanted his remains taken to the northern part of the U.S. He is one of the ghosts roaming the cemetery, a little angry about getting trapped in Cleveland for eternity. Visitors to the cemetery have seen him as a shadowy figure darting around. Legends tell that Joc-O-Sot was so furious that his burial was at Erie Street Cemetery, he made the earth shake, and his gravestone broke. A new marker replaces the old, but you can still see the shattered stone behind it.

Cuyahoga County
Jackass Hill
End of Praha Avenue
Cleveland, Ohio 44127
41.478804, -81.656823
Euclid Beach Park
16301 Lakeshore Boulevard
Cleveland, Ohio 44110
41.583997, -81.568897

Cleveland's Jack the Ripper -
The Mad Butcher of Kingsbury Run

Old "Jackass Hill" near the end of Praha Avenue and Kingsbury Run where a Cleveland shanty town was located during the Great Depression and became the hunting grounds for a killer.

Between 1934 and 1938, Cleveland was a gruesome playground for a mysterious serial killer called the Mad Butcher of Kingsbury Run. The murderer killed and dismembered in the least, a dozen shanty-town dwellers, drifters, and prostitutes, rivaling the murdering, mutilating romp of Jack the Ripper. Many of the bodies were discovered in Kingsbury Run, a slum section of the Cleveland area running along a creek ravine near railroad tracks.

The slayer began the carnage on the shores of Lake Erie and into Jackass Hill and ended the spree at the Lakeshore Dump. Unfortunately, authorities from around the U.S. never caught the criminal. Some believe the Mad Butcher's ghost still creeps through the city. Many think the spirits of the victims return to the places the killer dumped them. Whether you believe in the spooks or not, the horrible circumstances around the murders will send chills through even the most hardened souls.

Euclid Beach—On September 5th, 1934, the torso of a woman was found by a man walking the beach. She was later called *Lady of the Lake*. Others would report seeing her ghost stumbling along the shore.

Huron County

Blue Bridge
Township Hwy 118 (Lamereaux Road)
Norwalk, Ohio 44857
41.279413, -82.675063
Direction of Seymour Creek where the lights
are seen from the bridge:
41.280640, -82.676263

Dark Times at Seymour Creek and Blue Bridge

Blue Bridge along Lamereaux Road. Standing near the place where a murder occurred well over 200 years ago, and after, eerie little lights appeared along with an occasional apparition.

During the War of 1812, a blockhouse was built in Milan to protect area settlers from attacks by Indian raiders. When the fort was there, two young men—18-year-old Samuel Seymour and 15-year-old Reuben Pixley, Jr. set out from the blockade to cut down a bee tree and rob it of the honey and wax. They made their way to the tree's location on the south side of a small stream that met with the West Branch of the Huron River.

When they were just about finished with their job, they were fired upon by Indians. Seymour was instantly killed. Pixley got entangled in some brush as he tried to escape and was taken prisoner, where he remained in captivity for several months.

There is a little gravel pull-off before the Blue Bridge (aka Lamereaux Road Bridge) on the eastern side of the river. I parked there and walked across the expanse, watching to my right where Seymour Creek flowed into the West Branch of the Huron River. I paused as a fog rolled in at late evening. As I looked toward the point Seymour Creek flows into the river, I conjured up all kinds of ghostly images in my mind, the least being that of an apparition that could appear.

Later, the small creek where Seymour was killed would be named Seymour Creek. And this area where it meets with the West Branch of the Huron is haunted by Samuel Seymour. Early on, people taking Lamereaux Road and crossing the bridge, now called the Blue Bridge, over the West Branch of the Huron River would see little lights working their way through the valley where the young settler was murdered. Mist forms in the little pocket of the valley even during dry seasons, hazy lights dance along the banks and hillside where Samuel Seymour died, and some passing along the bridge have even seen the dark silhouette of a man there.

Wayne County

Chippewa Rogues Hollow Nature Preserve and Chidester Mill Museum
117514 Galehouse Road
Doylestown, Ohio 44230
40.941365,-81.67536

The Legends of Chidester Mill and Rogues Hollow

The Mill Museum in Rogues Hollow.

It is a mysterious place, the little valley along Silver Creek a couple of miles from Doylestown. When men first began mining there in the 1840s, folks started calling it Peacock Hollow due to the streaks of rainbow colors in the split coal seams. Then a doctor from Akron came in, bought up the mineral rights, and dubbed the valley Rogues Hollow. Since the 1840s, over 50 mines sprang up in the area along with five saloons.

It was quite a wild town with a storied past of tough coal miners, nightly bar-room brawls, and lawlessness. Many rowdy miners traveled Rogues Hollow roads like Fraze and Clinton to work and home and back again. Once in a while, the ghostly grind of wagon wheels and the clop of mule hooves ride the night wind. The spectral blast of dynamite explodes from afar. Even shadowy figures appear on the old roads that miners used to walk.

The Chidester Mill — the road was built up the hill and away from the mill to avoid the rowdy mine town.

Nearby Chidester Mill was a woolen mill, sawmill, and dye house started by Samuel and Ephraim Chidester. It was in business from 1828 to 1888 and passed down through the family. During its earlier years, a young man making repairs on the mill fell into the machine, and the wheel crushed him to death. Many living in Rogues Hollow said they saw him return at dusk, strolling the paths of the mill long after he was dead to complete his work. In 1922, the owners replaced the original building with the structure used as a museum today, and his ghost still strolls around.

A young woman was spurned by her sweetheart when he discovered she was pregnant. When the child was born, she walked to the bridge over Silver Creek near the mill and tossed the baby into the cold waters. If you stand on the bridge, you can hear the child's wails. And you might even see the mournful mama. She stands along the edge, staring into the water, crying desperately to get her baby back.

The Crybaby Bridge where a young mother sacrificed her baby, and its anguished cries are heard.

There was a legend about an old tree that grew on Clinton Road. It was called the Ghost Oak Tree because one night a tall horse galloping along the road collided with the tree and was killed. His ghost was seen under the tree for years, a dusky shadow beneath the limbs.

Wayne County

River Styx Trestle
256-262 E Ohio Avenue
Rittman, Ohio 44270
40.974941,-81.772252

Ghost Train Over River Styx

The trestle over River Styx in Rittman. Ghostly omen or just a ghost? You be the judge.

The Erie west-bound passenger train No. 5 was due in Mansfield at 8:56 a.m. on March 22nd, 1899. It was about a half-mile past Rittman and was heading toward Sterling at a rate of 60 miles per hour. Unfortunately, it did not make it on time. Sometime between 7:30 a.m. and 8:00 a.m., just as it crossed the trestle over a small stream named the River Styx (Styx River), the train jumped the track and rolled over. All the cars, barring a dining car, derailed. Alexander Logan, the 48-year-old engineer, was crushed beneath the train.

Seven months later, a local Rittman doctor was returning home with a friend after visiting a patient. Just outside town, the two leisurely watched a train working its way down the tracks. It was almost to the short trestle running over the River Styx when the shrill whistle caused them to turn. Just as it got to the trestle, they heard the engine engage as if it was being placed in reverse before it burst into flames and smoke spilled into the air. The crash of metal and wood rang out along with the crackle of broken trestle timbers and the hissing of escaping steam. Shrieks from the pinioned victims echoed from the wreckage. Then the sights and sounds dissolved as if the horrific train crash did not happen at all.

Over the next year, more people saw and heard the ghost train following its doomed path across the River Styx train trestle. By April of 1901, when townspeople reported seeing a train wreck occur when no genuine train was nearby, it rattled more than a few who believed it had to be some forewarning of dire disaster. But no calamity ever came. The town is alive and well. The river still runs beneath the trestle, and trains run above. And perhaps, on moonless nights, the sound of the No. 5 sometimes makes its fateful run along the tracks, and the screams still pierce the air.

Portage County

Elliot Family Farmstead & Cemetery
West Branch State Park
Cable Line Road (CR-120)
Ravenna, Ohio 44266
Cemetery: 41.129904, -81.127194
Trailhead: 41.129137, -81.126710
(Near Machine Trail)

Witch's Grave at Lost Cemetery

The spawning grounds of the Witch's Grave in Portage County.

The lonely ruins of the Elliott Family Cemetery at West Branch State Park are barely visible buried deep within the forest and along an almost-gone road. In the 1920s, when this graveyard was discovered by the Elliott Lake Club while clearing the land for a recreation area, it was called 'Portage's Lost Cemetery.' It was secreted ankle-deep in leaves and brush. Tree saplings had sprouted inside the hand-hewn sandstone fence surrounding the gravestones.

The abandoned cemetery was attached to the old farmstead of long-departed Mulford and Betsy Elliott back when it was not uncommon for folks to bury their dead not far from their backyards in family plots. Remnants of the home are hardly a stone's throw away across a creek running between. Among the tombstones was one steeped in tragedy marking the death of 17-year-old Glamenza Elliott with a gruesome epitaph etched into the face.

The Elliott Cemetery in 1963 before time and vandalism took a toll. *Image: Akron Beacon Journal-George Steinbeck leaning.*

She was not alone. Back in the 1920s, there were still at least seven gravestones from the Elliott family within the walls—Mulford Elliott (1801–1878) and his wife, Elizabeth "Betsy" Elliott (1801–1871), Wesley (1817-1817 at 1 1/2 days old), Malissa (1837 at 3 months old), John (1854-1854 at 10 months old) and teenaged Glamenza (1846-1864 at age 17). One more stone was still present, but the name was unreadable. Members of the Elliott Lake Club gallantly cleaned up the century-old cemetery on Cable Line Road, renewing the last traces of the family who once lived there.

But times would change, as would the land. After the U.S. Army Corps swooped up this little piece of countryside along with others for flood control, the State of Ohio built West Branch State Park with a reservoir in 1965. It was then that the property opened for public use. While the park was developing, it was not just hikers discovering the lonely graveyard and the skeleton of the old home. There were others with less respectful intentions who stumbled upon the solitary cemetery. They also found the old burial place of 17-year-old Glamenza and above it, the peculiar headstone with a poetic inscription doling out a haunting message of death and dying: *Remember youth as you pass by, As you are now, so once was I.* The morbid words come from an old Latin saying used by both Greeks and Romans in their epitaphs—*Quod tu es, ego fui, quod ego sum*— "What you are I once was, what I am, you will become."

Across the creek from the old Elliott Cemetery is the foundation of the home. Or is it? Some say that this was the stone that was laid atop the witch so she could not escape. And where ghastly red eyes peer out at those who peer in—

There was just something not right about the words on that grave. Surely they offered up a foreboding message. Just across the creek, too, there was a mysterious pile of stones. Now, everyone knew early settlers were intolerant of witches. Their ideal way of getting rid of them was to burn them to death and toss their ashes in the mud—well, after sewing the mouth shut, so they did not utter curses at those who were killing them. Like suicides, the God-fearing buried witches outside consecrated grounds with a slab of rock placed on top to keep them from climbing out of the grave as revenants, walking corpses that might harm those still living. Sometimes, they buried the wicked upside-down, so they would go in the wrong direction if they tried to dig their way out.

Or is this the slab of stones settled on the witch?

The curious heard the stories, and they sought the boneyard out searching for the witch grave. Instead, the old road became a secluded lover's lane for a boy to bring a girl and scare the bejeebus out of her. In the early years, rangers at the park tried to keep an eye on the cemetery, but in May of 1969, vandals desecrated the old graveyard. Headstones were broken and pushed callously to the dirt. Beer cans lay strewn across the old hallowed grounds.

After, there were claims that those who vandalized the cemetery came to all sorts of bad luck. Anyone who took something from the land met with some bad fortune. As the story goes, a witch's grave lies hidden in the forest. Legends tell that a young woman lay accused of being a witch. So those in town scooped her up and forced her into the woods. They laid her down, placed boards on top, then buried her beneath massive slabs of stones on top to kill her—and so she could not rise again. Now, you can see the ghostly form of the witch roaming the dark forest. If you peer into the depths of one slab of stone, dead-red eyes stare back at you.

The abandoned road once passing the Elliott farm and cemetery. At one time, there were homes all along this road. Now, only forest remains. Would you walk this road alone knowing that the ghosts of its past might still be around?

Now you know the legend of the witch's grave. But here is something that you should also know—fair warning. Something wicked might lie within. I mean, you cannot desecrate a cemetery and its graves and not expect a ghost or two to wiggle their way out of what they hoped was their eternal resting place and wreak havoc on those who pass by.

Many have visited the Witch's Grave. Regardless of the mundane reality of the cemetery, some have seen bizarre things, heard screams, and felt something touching them even during the day. A black figure skulks along the path and hides behind trees, watching those who pass.

At one time, people would take pieces of the stone pile laid atop the witch as souvenirs to show they had culled enough courage to hike to the witch's grave. Legends tell that those who did collect a little keepsake suffered misfortunes—from dying in car wrecks to just plain bad luck. Who would expect less—stealing from the dead? So my suggestion to those who visit—tread lightly. Do not defile or rob from the dead. Look from afar and maybe say a prayer. Or the deceased may come back in the most horrible, horrible ways to haunt you. Tonight. While you lay in bed. In the dark. Alone—*or maybe not so alone as you believe.*

Portage County

Grave of Chester Bedell
At Hartzell Cemetery
10450-10476 Canyo Drive
North Benton, Ohio 44449
40.996652, -81.010430

Snakes in a Grave

Grave of Chester Bedell where false rumors persisted for many years of snakes crawling around the plot.

At one time, this grave at Hartzell Cemetery in North Benton had a life-size bronze statue of a man crushing a scroll inscribed with SUPERSTITION beneath its left foot and holding another scroll high above its head with the right hand and UNIVERSAL MENTAL LIBERTY engraved on it. Crowds once flocked to the monument gazing upon the statue of the man, an outspoken atheist who loved to debate his opinion of religion. While they were there, they would search for snakes—

This large monument belonged to Chester Bedell. Through his life, Bedell studied the Bible and religion—not to find God, but to disprove the existence. He was quite a character, and it appears the folks in town took him like that with a shrug of shoulders and, perhaps, a groan when he showed up at the local church to tell his side of the story. Bedell loathed doctors and lawyers, contending they were serpents only out to rob their patron's earnings. He was well-traveled, and one of the wealthiest men in the county and was known to invite local preachers in for talk of theology—and a warm meal. Before his death at 81 in 1908 just after he had returned from a trip to the Holy Land, he had a life-size bronze statue made of himself proclaiming his beliefs.

A legend grew out of this man and statue twenty years after he was dead and buried. It was mostly from people outside of the community who had stumbled on his monument—evangelists looking for a hot sermon, profiteers looking to make a buck, and the devout looking for solid proof of their belief. They proclaimed that upon Bedell's deathbed, he shook a fist challenging God and declared: "If there be a God or any truth in the Bible, let my body be infested with snakes."

Hundreds flocked to the cemetery on Sundays, believing tales that told snakes were so thick when they buried Bedell that gravediggers and their shovels were utterly entangled. There were rumors that during Bedell's funeral, a sexton removed a snake from his grave, and after that, he had to take away snakes every day. Pamphlets and postcards circulated like wildfire with the story saying that those who visited watched as the ground pulsated with snakes, they crawled at the statue's feet, and made countless 'snake holes' surrounding the tomb.

Certain preachers were intent on proving it was true, so much so that they called anyone declaring the story unfound infidels and liars. Some even went into the weeds and scared a few poor snakes out, either stomped them to death with their shoes before tossing them by the grave, or they shoved them into a little glass jar to show their congregations the next Sunday what they had found.

An old caretaker discouraged the tourists visiting the grave—some had shot at it, and others tried to topple it to the ground—explaining there were no more snakes there than any other headstone. Townspeople denied the rumors, but then preachers accused the poor souls of being paid by the Bedell family for lying. People came in fevered hordes from all over the United States to witness the miraculous occurrence, see an atheist get his due.

Some who visited were not displeased—they saw the snakes. But look above—NO snakes. Back then, enterprising entrepreneurs paid children to collect snakes and place them on the grave, selling booklets and postcards to eager tourists. By the way, it is impossible for snakes to dig holes in the ground—they have no arms and legs to burrow. *No*, they do not use their snout to shove the dirt away. *Yes*, it is wicked to kill an animal to perpetuate a tale.

I dug through newspaper after newspaper, story after story about Hartzell Cemetery's infidel. One caught my eye—in July of 1938, the "Rambling Reporter" for the Pittsburgh Press, Ernie Pyle, had visited his family in Indiana. They told him the legend of the snakes related to them at a revival and Bedell's challenge to God to prove it by 'putting snakes in his grave.' His mother, a good Christian, told Pyle— "Fiddle-sticks, Ernest, I don't believe a word of it. Why don't you go there and write a column about it?"

Ernie Pyle did as his mother asked, finding himself standing in front of Chester Bedell's statue, then talking to locals as reporters tend to do. Old-timers did not recall any snakes in his grave. However, occasionally snakes would inadvertently wander from the woods and fields on to the carefully mown lawn as "a snake does not know a graveyard from a briar patch." And yes, people flocked there to stare at the grave, look for snakes. He also found that Chester Bedell had three children, his son was still living at the time at age 70. That people got so fanatic about Chester Bedell's beliefs, they shot at his statue, trampled the cemetery, and tore up the family plot. Preachers damned the man while standing over his grave and—

"On Saturdays, the little boys of North Benton catch snakes," Mister Pyle wrote, "and hang them over the Infidel's headstone. On Sundays, the tourists see the snakes and kneel and cry, 'Praise the Lord.' What would we do in this world without ornery little boys?"

Portage County

Rootstown Railroad Tracks
3242-3300 Industry Road
Rootstown, Ohio 44272
41.077852, -81.194114

Ghost Hollow

The tracks running by Ghost Hollow in Rootstown.

Railroad workers hated the run that crossed Industry Road in Rootstown along Ghost Hollow. A young boy by the name of Chapman drowned in one of the ponds near the railway there. His ghost would show up crying along the tracks. Rail men would stop the trains trying to help him, but workers found no boy around. If they saw the ghost, it meant bad luck would soon come.

Medina County

Spencer Cemetery
99 Jefferson Street
Spencer, Ohio 44275
41.101086,-82.122112

By the Lantern Light

An old-time lantern wiggles its way through the cemetery, held by spirited hands.

According to local lore, some have seen an old-fashioned lantern passing through the cemetery. Upon closer inspection, it appears held by ghostly fingers as it dangles there attached to no hands at all. At times, a second, tinier light joins along. Some stories relate that you can walk right up to the lamplight and pass your hands through it.

Mahoning County

Lanterman's Mill
Mill Creek Metroparks
1001 Canfield Road (SR-62)
Youngstown, Ohio 44511
Mill: 41.066806, -80.682140
Parking: 41.069119, -80.684629

Weeping Watcher of Lanterman's Mill

Lanterman's Mill in Youngstown. *Image: Mshake*

There is an old flour mill called Lanterman's Mill along Mill Creek in Youngstown. Passersby have witnessed a woman dressed in old-fashioned clothing peering out of the windows. Those who remember the story passed along to them divulge that during the Civil War, there was a young woman who worked in the mill whose fiancé was fighting for the Union. She would watch the bridge whenever soldiers would cross, hoping for his safe return. One day, a soldier came to her, but it was not her beloved. He disclosed her fiancé had died in battle. She died of grief not long after, but returns to watch out the window for her long-dead love.

Stark County

Lock 4 Park
Canal Fulton Heritage Society
6575 Erie Ave NW
Canal Fulton, Ohio 44614
40.877811, -81.583386

Old Fulton Lock Phantom Moans

The old Fulton or Lock 4—has a ghastly past.

Long ago, a worker was staying in the lock tender's cabin at Fulton Lock 4. He found out the lock would be closed as the railways began to take over as the mode of transportation. In a rage, he killed the other workers that day by pouring acid on them, then killed himself—all dying a slow death over the next week. Now their phantom moans and groans seep out of the area of Lock 4.

Geauga County

Punderson Manor Resort
11755 Kinsman Road
Newbury Ohio 44065
41.451257, -81.207584

Ghosts Hanging Out at Punderson Lodge

Punderson Manor Resort—beautiful and haunted. And a ghostly stay you do not want to miss out on.

Lemuel and Sibyl Punderson once operated a grist mill and distillery where Punderson Manor is located. Lemuel was 40-years-old when he died of malaria. W.B. Cleveland later owned it and, in 1929, sold the land to a millionaire hailing from Detroit named Karl Long. He began to build the 29-room mansion but died before completion. The manor eventually landed in the lap of the State of Ohio, and they finished the construction in the 1950s and started renting out the building to lodging guests.

Inside Punderson Manor Resort—where a ghostly apparition was seen hanging from the ceiling.

Many people have visited the building throughout the years, even before tourists entered the doors. Still, no one expected ghosts to pop up now and again. It was not long after it fell into the state's hands that strange things began happening at the inn. Several employees at the lodge were astounded one evening to find a ghostly apparition adorned in a flannel shirt hanging from a rope in the middle of the lounge. The image eventually vanished but remained there for hours. That is not all. Doors open and close, lights flicker, faucets turn off and on—annoyingly so often sometimes that staff has to step forward and tell the ghosts to stop. They do, at times, before they start again in a couple of days.

Park officers have been called to investigate reports of small children tearing up and down the hallways in the older part of the mansion. When they get there, no children are around. They also heard a woman's laughter when the building was closed for winter. There is a black cat with four white mitten paws that struts around the downstairs hallway. It is not living anymore. Reach out to pat its head, and it will probably disappear.

A park ranger making rounds within the building heard a spook's high-pitched, woman's cackle here.

Some wonder why ghostly children's laughter can be heard in hallways (below) when no known children lived in the building—but plenty of families lived around it even in 1857 when the map (left) was made.

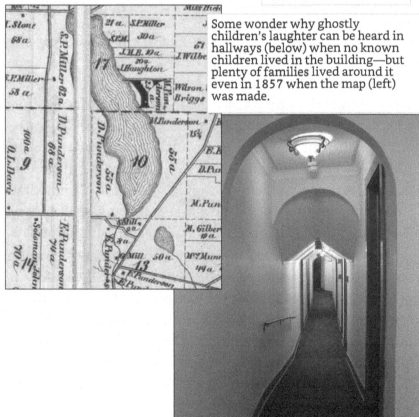

Holmes County

Salem Reformed Cemetery
Township Road 110
Millersburg, Ohio 44654
40.513669, -81.841397

Salem Cemetery Angel of Death

Just a mile from the small community of Saltillo, the Salem Reformed Church once stood along with its cemetery. Of the many graves at the church cemetery, one stands out among the others. It is a 15-foot tall monument topped with a 5-foot angel draped in drooping branches of evergreen. The angel was placed over the grave of Mary Conrad by her husband, George—a prosperous farmer with land south of the cemetery when she died at 57-years-of-age in April of 1890. Later, his family buried George beside her beneath the monument. After World War I, the congregation had grown older or scattered in many directions, and the church was eventually demolished. Now, only the lonely cemetery remains on the hilltop with the legendary angel, now headless.

In earlier years, folklore began to spread that this angel was an instrument of death; those who met her gaze at midnight would soon die. As a rite of passage, high school teens would gather as a group, daring each other to stand before the angel and waiting for her head to turn—whoever her eyes laid upon would die.

The angel now stands forlorn and vandalized over the years—her wings and hands broken. And her head is gone, stolen many times, but always returned as she tends to eke out little bits of revenge on those who hurt her. Once, police were investigating a fatal car crash, and when they opened the trunk of the vehicle, they found the angel's head—the teen who had stolen it ended up dead. Enough was enough—trustees secreted her head in a safer place. She is known to take to flight, and even with wings mangled, she flits around the cemetery in the dark.

Even though the Angel of Death has lost her head, her powers have not diminished. Now if you look up and see her head appear and she catches your eyes, you will die!

Harrison County

Tappan (aka Franklin)
86769-87057 Township Hwy 215
Scio, Ohio 43988
Mill Hill Cemetery:
40.358185, -81.208312
Tappan & Lake : 40.357040, -81.209267

Drowned Ghost Town —Raising the Dead

Welcome to the town of Tappan. Well, where it used to be. Now it is a ghost town—under water.

A lake covers the land where the tiny but thriving hamlet of Tappan once stood along the Little Stillwater Creek. It is eerie enough that those of meager means forced to leave recalled there was not enough time to take all from their homes before the U.S. Army Corps of Engineers dammed the water in the 1930s. As a result, much of the town remains beneath its watery grave—houses, mailboxes, and farm machinery once in a while observed by divers.

Tappan, a pretty town before the flooding.
Do ghosts walk below water now?

Families living there claim that although authorities moved a few graves from Tappan Cemetery to Mill Hill Cemetery on a hill above, not all those buried there were exhumes. Instead, their ghostly forms still rise from their tombs deep in the murky depths of Tappan Lake and go about their days. Passersby have watched the dead rise from Mill Hill Cemetery and shuffle down the roadway before vanishing into the lake.

Mill Hill Cemetery—Tappan Cemetery was allegedly moved here, but few graves stand.

Jefferson County

Old Panhandle Crossing
Steubenville, Ohio 43952

Shoots Ghost Every Night

near Steubenville, Ohio.

The place where ghosts would walk.

Patrick Hilley was a night watchman on the Panhandle Crossing in Steubenville. He swore every night, a ghost would walk the tracks, and he would shoot wildly at them with his revolver. His story went out in the newspapers from New Jersey to Kansas. And there were not any ghosts or people walking the tracks while he worked.

Summit County

Mary Campbell Cave
Gorge Metro Park
1160 Front Street
Cuyahoga Falls, Ohio 44221
Trail Head: 41.120552,-81.493367

Peculiar Haunting of Mary Campbell Cave

Mary Campbell Cave is haunted—ghostly voices are heard.

Mary Campbell was a 10-year-old girl from Pennsylvania kidnapped by Delaware Indians around 1758. Red-haired and freckle-faced, she was held captive at Chief Newcomer's village near Old Maid's Kitchen, a cliff overhang in Gorge Metro Park in Cuyahoga Falls. She was later returned to her family and died around 1801. Some say she spent time in the cave, thus the title is given—Mary Campbell Cave. Spirits of Indians and children, including a young girl like Mary with freckles and red hair, haunt the cave. Tiny lights dance along the trail. Cheerful whistling, children singing, and laughter echo through this recess cave.

Summit County

Bailey Road/Railroad Bridge at Gaylord's Grove
2672 OH-59
Cuyahoga Falls, Ohio 44221
41.145047, -81.472612
Parking: 41.145193, -81.473507

How William Beatson Lost His Head

The bridge where a dead man searches for his head.

It was a stormy Wednesday evening in April of 1853 when William Beatson came upon a large sum of money. Where the funds originated can be left to the imagination. Most likely, it was from thievery of some sort; although he was a butcher by trade, his reputation as a crook preceded him. Beatson persuaded a man named James Parks into taking a business trip to Pittsburgh with him.

James Parks was also a seedy character, spending time in jail in his homeland of England for poaching and grave robbery. He was a small-time criminal of about 35 years old, 5-foot and 6 inches tall, chubby, and missing his front teeth. Although never convicted of the crime, he murdered his common-law wife. At the time of the trip, he was managing a shabby saloon in Cleveland.

They never made it to Pittsburgh. The two got drunk, and sometime during their ride, the conductor made a call-out for a change of cars. Beatson and Parks boarded the wrong train in Hudson and got out at Cuyahoga Falls. Most likely, it was Parks's plan all along to rob Beatson during the trip. Before the two hopped off the Pittsburgh-bound train, Parks had made an excuse he needed to grab a cap in one of his bags and went through Beatson's luggage searching for cash. Finding no money, Parks would opt for a different route to steal Beatson's stash. Hence they 'accidentally' got off at Cuyahoga Falls. There, the two began to hit the taverns, and they argued whether to walk the eight miles back to Hudson or wait for another train.

Railroad Bridge over the Cuyahoga River at Gaylords Grove near Akron, Ohio. U. S. A.

A woman living near this bridge heard the sound of men tussling during the night.

The next morning, someone reported finding pools of blood near the train bridge at Gaylord's Grove. Not long after, the police located items under the bridge's abutment—a cane, bottle, and a cap found on a stump in a nearby field. Beatson's slashed clothing floated along the murky waters of the Ohio-Penn Canal. Authorities soon discovered his headless, naked body floating in the Cuyahoga River.

It was not difficult to trace the murder to James Parks, then find him in Buffalo, New York. A jury convicted Parks, and he was hanged for the crime. The long-time criminal had murdered Beatson and, hoping the man could not be identified without a head, took his dull-bladed knife and a stone, banged the knife tip through Beatson's neck until he cut off the head. He then threw the body into the river and the head into the canal. Parks paid for his crime. William Beatson should be able to rest in peace. Or so it would be thought. There was just one problem. No one ever found Beatson's head, so his ghost stands over the Bailey Road Bridge, staring down into the Cuyahoga River, looking for it.

The Cuyahoga River gently winds its way beneath a canopy of trees while a raft of mallards paddles lazily along— and a dead man might be seen peering over the bridge looking for his head.

Summit County

Hell Town
Stanford Road
Peninsula, Ohio 44264
41.277743, -81.549945

Highway to—Hell Town

The Highway to Hell in its more modern heyday. Even before, this road was known for thieves—as the hill dropped, carriage drivers could not see robbers lurking in the woods. Those murdered for whatever cash they carried still remain as ghosts.

The area dubbed Hell Town has been known as the old ghost town harboring Krejci Dump's industrial waste, the region that a massive python roamed the countryside, and the place of a crybaby bridge and a satanic church. Now it is part of Cuyahoga National Park. But long ago, old-timers described it as the place where the sad ghosts of murdered early travelers robbed by highwaymen staggered along the roadway.

Lorain County

Ruins of Swift Mansion - Light and Hope Orphanage
52374 Gore Orphanage Road
Amherst, Ohio 44001
41.355052, -82.335234

Gore Orphanage

The Swift Mansion—part of Light and Hope Orphanage aka "Gore Orphanage" before it burned down.

There is a story about an orphanage in Lorain County. While the children who lived there were sleeping in their beds, Old Man Gore, who ran the place, nailed all their doors shut. Then, he lit a match, caught the place on fire. Inside, the children awakened to a fiery death, tiny fists pounding on the barred windows and doors. Then they all went up in flames.

Well, not exactly. However, the story of one couple's greed and ruthless treatment of children who were really in an orphanage there was almost as wicked. In the early days, Johnathon Swift built a mansion on land along Gore Road (named for the triangular shape). It was later the home of the Wilber family, and after it caught the eye of John Sprunger, a wealthy industrialist/builder, and his wife, Katie. They chose the isolated property for a reason—they had a plan for an illicit, lucrative business venture and they did not want prying eyes to see what they were doing.

Right: Light and Hope Orphanage —Girl's quarters—

Left: Light and Hope Orphanage —Boy's quarters—

A capitalist at heart, Sprunger founded the Light and Hope Missionary Society in 1893 and the Light and Hope Orphanage. Around 1903, Sprunger purchased the Hughes farm in Amherst and three other neighboring farms, including Howard's farm and buildings, to house children. Here, the Sprungers established the printing shop and publishing company under the guise of an orphanage trade training center for children. The children, ranging from seven to seventeen, were indentured servants—forced to do free work providing services in the printing company and working the farm. Sprunger also rented the children out for agricultural work as farmhands to surrounding farms.

His scheme was not new—children had been bought from Victorian workhouses and overworked without wages in exchange for board and food as pauper apprentices in England since the 17th century. To the public eye, he posed as a saint; his undertakings had all the appearances of a training facility where teachers taught boys a trade and girls learned domestic sciences. In reality, the children were victims of Sprunger's capitalist greed with the deceptive outward appearance of evangelism and charity.

The boys lived at the Hughes farm, and the girls dwelt at the old Howard farm. The children's overseers lived at the Swift Mansion. Light and Hope Orphanage would eventually encompass over 500 acres. A 1910 U.S. census shows forty-five people were living on the property, including twenty-seven children, Katie and John Sprunger, and fifteen helpers and assistants. In actuality, sources state there could have been up to 125 children on the property at a single time. The caretakers were not caregivers at all but wardens/overseers for the laboring children. Sprunger treated children like slaves, and he got richer and richer.

The Swift Mansion before burning to the ground. Note the post to the right. It is the only remnant still standing today.

The complaints and investigations of abuse and slave labor at the farms plagued the orphanage from the onset. It came to a head in 1909 when children began to run away and tell local, empathetic Amherst townspeople about their abuse. It got so bad that nearby townspeople established an underground railroad for escaping children. When they worked, beatings were a common form of punishment to the children by both overseers, the Sprungers, and local farmers. The Sprungers also forced their slave labor to eat spoiled food. Bedbugs, lice, and rats were commonplace in their cots at night. A sick cow found dead in a field was used for the children's meals. Instead of a doctor's care and medicines, they called upon prayer for healing. The orphanage, by judge ruling, was placed into different hands.

So it was true that a cruel, horrible man ran the orphanage. And there was also a fire during the time that authorities investigated the orphanage over allegations of abuse—in 1910, a boxcar filled with oil and printing supplies burned. It was a three-story building destroyed used for the printing of the Sprunger's Light and Hope Magazine. It exploded so heartily that flames filled the sky. There is no mention in newspapers of children killed during the explosion or fire, nor is there mention that authorities investigated to check for foul play or deaths. Records of the number of children at the orphanage were poorly kept and rarely accurate.

Although the large fire killing hundreds of children may not be confirmed, there are ghosts of its past. The orphanage stayed open until 1916. The old mansion was burned down in 1923 by homeless taking up residence. People did die here—two of the initial owners, the Swift children, are buried in the Gore Orphanage/Andress family cemetery. There are probably a few settlers who died here even earlier.

At least one orphan boy died nearby, 'coasting' on the back of a car. And those old, disturbing memories still linger of cruelty on the property to sad little orphans who may have returned to the place to haunt Old Man Sprunger and his hired hands for their beatings and slavery.

There have been tales of a ghost child swinging on an old tree. And while carrying a recorder at Gore Orphanage, I heard a child's voice say softly "Tryphenia"—that is how I found out about the Swift's children, researching what the word meant and finding it was a name of their 5-year-old daughter, Tryphenia, who died at age five in 1831.

It is worth the hike beneath the trees to search out the foundation, find the old well, imagine what it looked like before fire burned the mansion to the ground. Some put baby powder on the back of their car to see the tiny handprints show up. Try it. Maybe, you will see the ghost of someone's past like thousands before you. Because they say they have.

Little remains but buckled foundation and cornerstones—and this hitching post/gate post. And yes, a few ghosts!

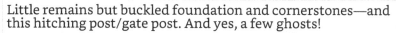

Old hitching post-

Lorain County

Bridge Over Vermilion River
52299 Twp Hwy 34
Vermilion, Ohio 44089
41.360009,-82.334296

Gore Orphanage Crybaby Bridge

Park before this bridge and you might find tiny, ghostly handprints on your car!

Just past the ruins of Swift Mansion, a bridge crosses the Vermilion River. This span is near the location of the actual orphanage buildings—cottages for girls and boys. Some see mists and lights at the bridge. Those who park their cars in the gravel pull-off before the bridge and turn off their vehicles have gotten small, dusty handprints on their car windows and windshield. And the sound of children crying can be heard when driving away.

Carroll County

Minerva Ohio 44657

About that Lost Frenchman's Gold and Monsters

Rolling into the town of Minerva where Bigfoot and gold have become great quests for treasure and monster hunters alike.

For the curiosity-seeker, the little town of Minerva is known for two things—a Bigfoot-like monster who visited a family in the 1970s and a lost treasure of gold. Now, about the beast—all seven feet of a huge, hairy thing showed up in August of 1978 stinking of ammonia and lurking behind the Cayton family home on the outskirts of town. It visited them for several nights and then faded away with occasional sightings but caused something of a national Bigfoot craze.

Some still see the creature that showed up along the roadways and scared folks around town for a while until they realized it would not hurt anybody. But as far as the treasure in Minerva—it has not shown up. So here are the particulars of the lost gold culled from a variety of sources so perhaps you can go on your quest. Many disagree on the specific details of its placement, but certainly, all agree that it is still out there unfound—

During the French and Indian War, George Washington led nearly 2000 British Troops to overtake Fort Duquesne. Indians speedily warned their French allies that an attack on their fort was imminent, and 16 packhorses loaded with gold and silver for the military payroll were removed from Fort Duquesne before it fell in 1758. The soldiers were to bury the treasure should they be overcome by the enemy and mark the concealment spot. They fled westward toward a blockhouse with provisions at Bolivar along the route of the Great Tuscarawas Trail that was the main path between the French Fort Duquesne and Detroit.

The British were successful in taking the fort. Three days later, the soldiers fleeing with the gold sighted an enemy's advance guard catching up to them along the Great Trail. The officer in charge told the men to dig a hole, unload the packhorses of their burden of gold, and bury it. They covered the hole with earth, then leaves and branches. At the same time, the British attacked, and only two Frenchmen survived with knowledge of the gold and the location.

In 1829, one of the nephews of the two French soldiers who survived found, among his uncle's belongings, a letter detailing the story of the treasure and written by Henry Muselle, a survivor. He began to search for the gold. As he made his way, he relayed his own story to the locals around Minerva with the clues given to find the treasure.

There were specific landmarks—the gold was buried centrally to four springs that came together, forming an odd square. About a mile west of this burying spot, an oddly shaped rock was jammed into the fork of a tree by Muselle. As they left to the East, a figure of a deer was carved into a tree one mile east of the gold. The soldiers' shovels to bury the treasure were concealed beneath logs nearby and would still be there.

The nephew was unsuccessful in his search and left, although it stirred up many curious people who also wanted to find the gold. But when no one discovered it, the desire to search it out eventually died down. It was not until many years later that on April 3rd, 1875, the Minerva Commercial reported the story of the treasure along with its clues. And those living in the area recalled they had unknowingly discovered those signs that matched the directions—when one farmer was cutting trees for rails, he cut one tree and found an odd-shaped stone wedged inside the trunk, and the tree had grown around it. Another man spoke up and said he might have a clue—lightning had struck a tree on his property, peeling back the bark, which exposed within a deer carved into it. And another man found old muskets and artifacts buried near an old shed.

Once again, people flocked to Minerva in the wild pursuit of gold. And again, treasure-hunters came up empty-handed. As time passes, once in a while, people get enthusiastic about searching it out, but so far as it is known, no one has ever found it. And the legend still lives on.

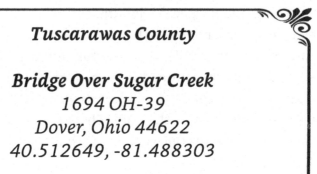

Tuscarawas County

Bridge Over Sugar Creek
1694 OH-39
Dover, Ohio 44622
40.512649, -81.488303

Ghost of Sugar Creek

Mary Seneff

The bridge over Sugar Creek where a ghostly girl would appear after her murder by a jealous wife.

In June of 1880, Canal Dover resident John Krause stared at something akin to a sack floating in the calm waters of Sugar Creek when he crossed the bridge along Shanesville Road heading toward his job at the coal mines. Curious, he drew off his boots and sloshed through the muddy water. Then he towed the object shoreward with a piece of rail until he saw what he thought was a striped coverlet sewn into a sack. Not wanting to open the bag, the man released it to the water's current and continued to work.

Krause mentioned his find to the other men, and it was not long before he and a few workers, including another miner, William Deiser, would travel back to Sugar Creek to investigate. There, the miners hauled the peculiar package to shore while curious bystanders watched. Those who stood by leaned forward inquisitively as fingers loosened the sack that was lazily tied together, then covered their noses with cupped hands as the stench of something decomposing filled their nostrils. Then the material unfolded to reveal walnut shells, a calico dress, ashes, a brick, and a partially dressed, badly beaten corpse. In the center, there was a darkened, rotting-skinned skull stuffed indiscriminately against some clothing.

Authorities quickly identified the remains as 18-year-old Mary Seneff. She had been missing for over two weeks, and her sister, Sarah Resler, had visited recently and voiced her concerns to local authorities of the girl's absence. Mary had come to work as a domestic servant cleaning the family homes of David Crites and his son-in-law Henry Athey who lived in houses on the same property on Stonecreek. She also helped Henry's wife, Ellen, who had suffered a miscarriage that year and needed help with the home and children. Among their houses was a small community of close-knit families related in one way or the other by blood or marriage—the Fishers, the Crites, and the Atheys. Mary's mother and father settled in Indiana, but her family had once lived in the area, and her married sister, Sarah Resler, still resided in the nearby village of Barrs Mills.

However, early in June, Sarah had gotten a letter from Mary stating she had left to visit her mother in Indiana. Not only did a misspelling of Mary's last name tip Sarah off as being peculiar, but it was also unusual for the woman to go without notice to her sister beforehand—the two were quite close. The Atheys maintained Mary had left for another job .

Along with local authorities, the constable paid a visit to the Crites's farm on June 16th. A horrid odor oozed from the backyard. The men followed it to a five-foot ash heap and began to dig in the charred residue. Some cabbage stalks, calico soiled with blood, walnuts, bricks, and a rubber garter were within. Next, they went to a wagon in the barnyard and found it was wet and muddy and held coal ashes. There was an ax also in the carriage with blood on the head. Inside the home, they found shoe buttons in the stove and stationary with handwriting matching fraudulent letters sent to Mary's sister stating the young domestic servant had left for her mother's home.

Ellen Athey was arrested and jailed. She confessed she had committed the crime in a jealous rage, believing young Mary was making passes at her husband. She had a dream Mary was having an affair with her husband, and the jealousy slowly began to nibble away at her sanity. Ellen murdered poor Mary with an ax and buried her in the yard. But the stench of the body decomposing bade her ask her family to help her dispose of it farther away. The body was dug up, wrapped in material, and weighted down with bricks before tossing it into Sugar Creek. The arrest of her husband, Henry Athey, and brothers 24-year-old Alexander and 16-year-old Frank Crites came directly after for helping her dispose of the body. It would be several months before Alexander and Henry were released. Only Ellen went to trial.

Mary's ghost began to show up where the men tossed her body over the old iron bridge above the Sugar Creek. It was not just one, but many who saw a misty form in the water rise up and take the shape of a woman so clearly, she was recognizable. Mary's ghost would try to address some with arms open wide. Others, she passed, walking from the bridge and toward the home where the murder took place.

Columbiana County

Beaver Creek State Park
Hambleton's Mill
Sprucevale Road
Negley, Ohio 44441
40.706864, -80.580722

Ghosts of Old Sprucevale

"In the deserted stone mill at Sprucevale, on St. Nicholas eve, the ghost of Esther Hale, the Quaker Lady preacher, appears and rewrites on the stone wall her old text 'Come.'" *From Ira Mansfield; Robin Hood Club. Little Beaver River valleys, Pennsylvania —Ohio with illustrated check list of flowers and essays. 1914.*

Esther Hale—

In the early 1800s, the Hambleton brothers—James, Charles, Benjamin, and Isaac purchased a grist mill and platted out the town of Sprucevale, which, at its peak, had about 12 homes with 20 families. The 73-mile Sandy and Beaver Canal ran through the town boasting a grist mill, pottery shop, woolen factory, store, post office, warehouses, and a blacksmith shop.

The community thrived until 1847, when the canal boom years waned with the coming of the railroad and the lack of funds to sustain it. So reliant was the town upon the canal that when it declined, the people and the buildings began to fade away too. By 1870, Sprucevale was not much more than a printed name on a map.

The grist mill remains today, and it is home to a ghostly woman named Esther Hale. Hale came from Carmel Church of the Orthodox Friends. She was among the first of these robust Pennsylvania preachers, a hard worker who toiled among the Sandy and Beaver Canal laborers. She was a tough old bird, frugal, and advised temperance among the rowdy canal men who liked to imbibe in a few drinks after a hard day of work. Whenever Hale would preach, she would call out for those in her audience: "Follow me down the path to salvation!" Now on St. Nicholas's Eve, December 5th of each year, the ghost of Preacher Hale appears at the old Hambleton grist mill dressed in white. She scratches "Come" on the wall of the old stone grist mill before she leads those watching inside and vanishes.

Gretchen's Lock—

According to old archives, E.H. Gill was the chief canal engineer and a graduate of the Royal Engineer's School in Paris. He traveled from France along with his wife and 7-year-old daughter, Gretchen, to help build the Sandy and Beaver Canal. Unfortunately, tragedy struck halfway to the United States when Gill's wife was washed overboard and drowned. Grief-stricken, the father and daughter continued to their new life. Gill would get a job with the Sandy and Beaver Canal system and help build the lock above Sprucevale. His daughter followed him from camp to camp, living in the wild area around the new canal.

During this time, Gretchen contracted malaria. One afternoon as her fever mounted, she made her father promise to take her home and bury her with her mother—"I want to join my mother," she pleaded. Wanting to please her, the father nodded that indeed, he would. But, before the day ended, Gretchen was dead.

Gretchen's Lock at Beaver Creek State Park.
Parking at picnic area close to trail: (40.704946, -80.585227)
Gretchen's Lock: (40.7078408, -80.593682)

Temporarily, workers prepared a crypt in the masonry of Lock 41 just above Sprucevale, and Gretchen was entombed in a small casket there. A major recession in the U.S. economy occurred in 1837, and Gill resigned his position to return to Europe. Gretchen's body was taken from her interim tomb in the lock and placed on the ship to return home with her father for reburial. However, the vessel that Gill was sailing on was lost at sea during a storm on the return voyage. He and Gretchen would join her mother just as she begged him to do. Still, Gretchen returns to the lock once in a while, murmuring her dying prayer, "Bury me with my mother."

Ashtabula County

Cederquist Park
Railway Iron Bridge Over Ashtabula River
Harmon Hill Road
Ashtabula, Ohio 44004
Park: 41.875201,-80.782753
Site: 41.878333,-80.789577

Spirits of the Ashtabula Train Wreck

Horror Upon Horror newspapers flashed across their front pages in exclamation of the wreck. And then came the ghosts. The disaster as illustrated in Harper's Weekly—January 20th 1877.

On the wintry evening of December 29th, 1876, a snowstorm blasted through northern Ohio, leaving a thick, two feet of snow on the ground in the village of Ashtabula. Winds were gusting a chilly 40 miles per hour. The Pacific Express No. 5 of the Lake Shore and Michigan Southern Railway moved westward across the tracks toward the bridge. It was going a mere 15 miles per hour, heading toward the depot only 3/10 mile away.

There were approximately 159 crew and passengers on board, many traveling for the holidays. It was a diverse passenger list of men, women, and children, both young and old, families and businessmen—some onboard had families waiting for them in Ashtabula, others across the U.S. in California. William Clemens of Bellevue was returning home from selling hogs in Buffalo, New York. Eighteen-year -old Effie Neely and her boyfriend were returning from a trip to Niagara Falls. Philip Bliss, a professional songwriter (he wrote 100 hymns including Let the Lower Lights Be Burning), and his wife Lucy traveled to their home in Chicago. Harry Bennet was along for the ride, a salesman who sold newspapers and other trinkets to train riders.

The train had two locomotives and 11 cars—two baggage cars, two-day passenger coaches, two express cars, a smoking car, a drawing-room car, and three sleeper cars. It had departed New York the day before, heading east. Only a bridge over the Ashtabula River came between the passengers and their destinations. It would not seem such a feat for the train to safely traverse the 65-foot span of the bridge like so many trains before. But there was something not quite right with the bridge, something that had gone undetected even during inspections. Years earlier, a tiny crack in a small air hole had grown with the weight of trains going across the bridge, forcing a brittle fracture in the structure. The frigid temperatures and the heaviness of the train caused too much stress on the poorly built system. Just as the lead engine cleared the west bank, the bridge collapsed, leaving the rest of the train to plunge into the river and bank below. It was a 70-foot fall into the frozen waters. When the train hit bottom, oil lamps and coal heating stoves in the railcars ignited, and the cars burst into flames.

William Clemens was hurt and later died from his injuries. Philip Bliss worked his way from the wreck to find his wife still pinned beneath the carriage. He stayed with Lucy in the burning wreckage, and they both died in flames. Harry Bennet would live. A rescuer pulled Effie Neely from the wreckage just as the cars went up in flames. Her boyfriend died trying to save others. Effie died in 1960 at the age of 101, the last survivor of the Ashtabula Disaster.

Of the 159 passengers and crew onboard the Pacific Express No. 5, 64 were injured, and 98 died. Forty-eight of those who died were unidentifiable—crushed by the train or burned alive by the flames. It was a horrifying moment in history for Ashtabula and the families who lost their loved ones. However, time would pass, and new laws for bridge design were made due to the disaster. And sometimes, people hear the cries of those who perished. Other times, shadows trudge around the area of the ravine just below the new bridge. They form around the region the train once fell in full attire and stand to stare where they lost their lives.

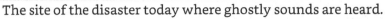

The site of the disaster today where ghostly sounds are heard.

Trumbull County

Rock Ridge Cemetery and Roads Along the Pennsylvania/Ohio Border

225 N. State Line Road
Greenville, Pennsylvania 16125
Along OH-88 Roadway:
41.387177, -80.528676 to
Rock Ridge Cemetery:
41.41030, -80.51420

Mysterious Shine

Rock Ridge Cemetery—where a tragical story of star-crossed lovers begins and ends.

In the mid-1800s, the Ohio towns of Burgh Hill and Vernon along Trumbull County's Pennsylvania border were growing villages with prosperous farmers. John Harbush was such a man who had a farm along the road just outside Vernon, Ohio. He had a daughter, Mary, who was very pretty. It was only the two of them—father and daughter as his wife had died years before. Mary was kind and giving. Those who knew her said when you looked into her bright eyes, she was so beautiful inside; you could see the brilliant shine of her soul.

John Harbush was quite protective of his only child. Many men wished to court her; however, her father had already chosen a husband for the young woman. This man was suitable, in John's eyes, as he was wealthy and had many cattle. Moreover, being much older than Mary, he would care for her with his wealth of experience.

But Mary had fallen deeply in love with Richard Lewis, an outgoing, popular schoolteacher from Pennsylvania. Few knew of their love. But if someone caught them sneaking a peek at each other, they could see their eyes sparkle with passion between them, a certain bright glow lighting up the young faces. Each night, after everyone went to sleep, the couple would sneak out and meet at a hilly meadow near a little graveyard, Rock Ridge Cemetery, just over the state line. The sweethearts were destined for tragedy; it was not long before the man who had been chosen by her father to court Mary found out the secret affair. Mary's husband-to-be stormed into the home of John Harbush, demanding the young couple break off the relationship. John bade the angry man be patient; he would deal with the situation.

Rock Ridge Cemetery—the place where the young lovers met.

And such, John did. He waited out his time, watched his daughter leave the house one night, following along Burgh Hill-Vernon Road, then to Greenville before she turned along State Line Road. Mary slipped furtively past the little Rock Ridge Cemetery, stepping lightly up the path to a tiny hillock. When she and Richard lovingly embraced, John Harbush saw the twinkle in both their eyes, a loving glow that seemed to gush from their very souls. Enraged, he rushed forward, striking Richard hard on the head with a stick. Mary's sweetheart died immediately from the massive gash in his skull, the blood gushing along his neck and jacket until his eyes dulled in death. In disbelief and agony, Mary sank to her knees next to her love, moaning and screaming. Shock overwhelmed her, and the young woman fell senseless in a heap atop the dead man. She, too, appeared to lose that shine, her eyes suddenly lackluster and listless.

John Harbush quickly dragged the dead teacher into the brush and made a shallow grave with his bare hands, covering the body with dirt, brush, and leaves. He carried his daughter home in his arms, an unmoving body as lifeless as her sweetheart. When Mary awakened the next morning, her hair was frost-white. She never spoke of the murder and refused to talk at all. She barely ate and began to waste away quickly. Her eyes, once full of spirit, were dull.

She died only a few months later and took the horrid murder to her grave. After the death of his daughter, John Harbush took to drinking. His farm fell into complete disrepair, and he, too, died within the year. On his deathbed, though, he confessed to murdering his daughter's beloved Richard Lewis. Yet, he did not divulge to anyone where he buried the man.

People knew. Because in the winter of 1882, farmers along the Pennsylvania and Ohio border began to see an eerie, brilliant light twice the size of a lantern flame.

It started with a pretty, sky-blue tint and other times, a bright red or even yellow color. It flit and floated, gently gliding over the hill alighting on the grave of the murdered schoolteacher, but always it returned within the bounds of the cemetery.

The route along roads and fields the little light traveled and where two young lovers' feet would tread to meet in secrecy until death knocked at their doors.

The first time it was seen, a family was returning from church and believed it was someone carrying a lantern and taking a shortcut home through their property. One farm lady followed the mysterious shine into the woods behind the cemetery before it completely disappeared, frightening her enough she made quickly for home. After some time, trying to solve the mystery, each farmer was armed with a bell, and when they saw the strange glow, they would take the bell and shake it wildly until the others followed suit, hoping to surround and capture the light. But just like John Harbush could never really douse the loving glow spilling from the two young lovers' hearts, the farmers never caught the mysterious shine either.

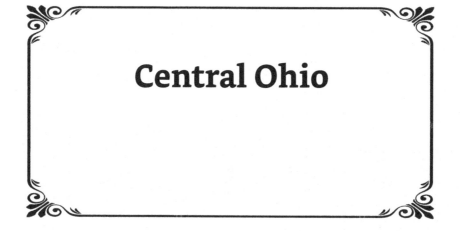

Central Ohio

Coshocton County

Stockum Graveyard
AEP/ODNR Public Hunting Area
County Road 123A
Coshocton, Ohio 43812
40.210370, -81.779505

Mary Stockum's Grave(s)

Stockum Cemetery (AKA Saint Johns Lutheran Church Cemetery)

Teens have taken the journey to search for Mary Stockum's grave for more than 50 years in the dark. They come to look for the two graves of the ghost of the woman wandering around the Saint Johns Lutheran Church Cemetery, searching for her head. Local folklore says there was once a lady named Mary Stockum who lived nearby. She had nine children. One of them was mentally disabled, and one day, her husband decided to kill the child and, so, he did. He was caught, convicted, and hanged for his crime.

In revenge for the hanging, Mary began killing off her children one by one. After the fifth one died, she too was brought to justice and was killed for her crimes. Then she was buried within the confines of the cemetery next to her husband.

Before she died, though, she cursed the land and the people around the community and said the rest of her children would die along with her, then one by one those in the town would die too. Everyone thought the horror was over, that her curse was just the rant of a crazy woman. But the remaining children she had not murdered did not recover. One by one, they began to die. When the sixth child passed away and fearing the worst, the townspeople dug up Mary. They severed her head from her body and left it in a shallow grave outside the boundaries of the cemetery, praying that it would break what they were sure now was a witch's curse. Then they plopped one gravestone on the mound above her body and one over her head. Now, she returns around the old ruins of the graveyard in ghostly form stumbling between the two headstones desperately searching for her head so she can complete the curse.

Mary Stockum's grave (s).

You can find the legendary graves. It is a long, pothole-ridden, muddy drive, then a mucky walk through an AEP/ODNR public hunting area. There are cliffs and drop-offs, ruts, twists, and two turns to the road appearing to stop in the middle of nowhere. The mud churned up by ATV-running hunters on the archaic County Road 123 is seasonally ankle deep in some parts, knee-deep in others. But between, there is a small hillock with graves that time, vandals, and trees have knocked to the ground. Among them, you will find a couple of headstones—one with the name Anna Mary Stockum who was the wife of Christopher Stockum. The two owned a 315-acre farm around Bacon and the area the cemetery sits upon now. They had emigrated from Hessen, Germany, by ship in 1836, a grueling eighteen-week trip on the Brig Aurora, and they came without a penny in their pocket. The couple spent much of their lives pushing back the wilderness on their plot in Linton Township and building the land, which later was a valuable farm.

The 1860 census shows the Stockums had seven children living in the home—Mary-18, Adam-17, Elizabeth-15, John-13, Martin-12, Caroline-11, Jacob-9. By 1870, all the children still appeared to be living. An eighth child, Solomon-9, was also listed in the household in the census. Adam, the eldest son, had returned from the Civil War to help farm the land. Caroline was the eldest daughter, and she maintained the home. Only one person is missing – Anna Mary, the mother. She had passed August 29th, 1863. In late August of that year, there were several other known deaths from people in the tiny community buried at the church cemetery. Was it merely some sort of flu epidemic? Or is there more to the story lost in time?

There are two sides to the story—one that shows on paper the family of Mary Stockum was a typical family.

They lived. They died and their bodies buried in a family plot on their land in Linton Township. They had neighbors by the name of Apple and Gosser, some of which are buried in the cemetery too. There is also a tale told by word of mouth, by story passed down from one to another. It is more exciting, more gruesome, and a tale of a crazy witch buried after killing her young. There are scores of eye-witnesses from hunters to adventure-seekers who have seen the filmy apparition of Mary, heard her screams, been terrified by the ghostly apparition walking the cemetery.

A gravestone belonging to Mary Stockum.

An article in the November 11th, 1967 Coshocton Tribune by Joanna Ross points out the legend was begun by the sight of two gravestones for Mary, hence one for the body and one for the head. A local caretaker verified it was true. However, his reason was a lot less horrifying and had a more prudent explanation. Yes, there were two gravestones for Mary. The original gravestone was replaced by a newer one. The old headstone was plopped up next to the fence for lack of a better place to put it. Now the question is: which of the two stories do you believe?

Will you pass the story off as local folklore, roll your eyes, and chuckle a little beneath your breath at those who, over the past century, believed the rumor? Or will you take the more adventurous position and trek into the woods like many before you, see if you can verify the ghost of Mary Stockum and listen for the screams?

Because there really was a Mary Stockum, and she really did die and was buried there. Hundreds of people swear they have seen her ghost, heard her yowls. They will tell you that something is there deep in the woods at the old cemetery. If you do visit, the area is hazardous. It is along a former strip mine, and there are cliffs and drop-offs. The road is rutted and muddy. You may hear screams, many have. You may see a milky white form along the way as some have sworn to have seen. And there could, quite possibly, be something more dangerous lurking. There are always secrets buried beneath the dirt along with the dead in ghost towns long gone with no one still living to tell us the truth of what went on that hot August summer deep in the farmland and forests of Coshocton County.

(AEP/DNR public areas have rules and regulations. Many include day-use activities only. However, unless you are looking for vampires, you should have no problem searching for the unknown during daylight hours. And please, many of the graves have been knocked over by trees, vandals, and weather. Respect the dead and those who are still living who might have known them) Seasonally, you may need to park near the intersection of County Road 123 (on the right) and 123A (left)— (40.209008, -81.785404). Take 123A to the left, walking the .4 mile back to the cemetery along the old roadway. The road curves, but it is a straight walk to the graveyard, which is on the right (40.210353,-81.779499) and within sight of the roadway. Not a suggested walk at night! There are probably day-use only restrictions.

Ashland County

Tunnel Bridge
1300 Township Road 1536
Ashland, Ohio 44805
40.83909, -82.37880

Ghostly Push

The Haunted Tunnel on Township Road 1536.

There are almost as many legends associated with this tunnel as there are generations who have visited it. One story goes like this: Children began to disappear at an alarming rate in a small Ohio farming community outside Ashland. Folks knew it was a witch who used them in her ritual sacrifices. Outraged, the farmers hunted her down and hung her in a bridge tunnel. Now, if you drive through the tunnel, stop, turn off your lights, and put your car in neutral, ghostly hands will push your vehicle to the opposite end. You can do this night or day. (Of course, I do not recommend this stunt. It is a road that still has traffic.)

Crawford County

Dead Man's Hollow
1601 Ohio 19
Bucyrus, Ohio 44820
40.762406,-82.875649

True Story of Dead Man's Hollow

On September 28th, 1836, a man was murdered in this hollow. After, his ghost has been seen along the roadway.

In September of 1836, John Hammer and his brother-in-law, Daniel Bender, traveled by foot from Pennsylvania over the Allegany Mountains and to Wooster, Ohio. Daniel, the younger of the two, was only 25-years-old and was along for the grand adventure, to see a part of the world he had never seen before. He was unmarried and carried about $30.00, spending money in his coat pocket. His companion, John, was 45-years-old and married to Daniel's sister, Catherine. He had a bit more money in his hands, about $200.00, which he would use to purchase land.

They paused in Wooster long enough to stop at the bank, then set off to Galion, where they visited a grocery store. There, they met a pair of men who offered to journey with John and Daniel from Bucyrus onward for both company and protection, as they were going in the same direction.

As the four men worked their way across the swampy ground outside of Olentangy, the new men began to spar who could carry the most massive walking stick. When they came upon a marshy section and a smaller creek that flowed into the larger Whetstone Creek, John and Daniel took two separate but parallel paths. Each was followed by one of the two men they had met in Galion. Then, the two newcomers attacked Daniel and his brother-in-law from behind. One drew his pistol and shot Daniel in the back of the head. John was struck with the huge stick by the second man.

John regained consciousness and was able to flag down help at a local sawmill. However, he did not speak English, and it was later before a stranger traveling the roadway found Daniel's lifeless body. John Hammer did recover and purchased land in Crawford County. But it is his brother-in-law whose memory has survived the longest—the place of his death given the nickname Dead Man's Hollow.

Daniel Bender's ghost walks where he died. Legend states a man was trying to get his young daughter to a doctor in Bucyrus by carriage sometime later on the same route Daniel and his brother-in-law had traveled. A deathly pale stranger hailed him from the road, and the man impatiently pulled over. Upon looking at the little girl bundled in a blanket, the stranger introduced himself and said that the child would not live to the morning. Disconcerted, the father snapped his reins and took off down the road. However, when the little girl died that night, the father swore the man who had given the forewarning was none other than Daniel Bender.

Fairfield County

Old Logan Road
Old Logan Road SE
Sugar Grove, Ohio 43155
39.617564, -82.553192

Dead Peddler Detour

The road where a dead peddler would jump out at passing carriages—and later, more modern vehicles.

Old Logan Road in Sugar Grove between Lancaster and Logan has been known for 200 years as haunted. It was right around 1815 when the ghostly form appeared, scaring away carriage riders and farmers traveling this main road. Back then, Sugar Grove was little more than a few cabins dotting the hillsides and not the pretty village it is now. Pierre Bordeau, of French descent, made himself comfortable in a shabby, little place by the road. It was along the hillside not far from the location the Sharp family sells pumpkins around Halloween these days.

It would be Pierre's shack that a peddler would stop and ask for a night's sleep along his route. But over the next few days after, those who usually bought from the peddler noted he had not visited their homes. Many believed he had probably left Pierre's cabin during the night, so he did not have to pay for his lodging. No signs would call up an alarm of any foul crime save a small pool of blood found by a spring near the road.

Years would pass, and rumors always kept travelers away from Pierre's cabin. Nobody wanted to stay there for rest. The water in the spring tasted bad, and there were stories of a ghost haunting the road and hillside. It popped out at carriage riders taking the Logan Road route, the only rugged path that once ran a straight drive from Lancaster to Logan. It disappeared at the old spring.

Of course, no one suspected Pierre of murder. On the contrary, he was considered kind-hearted and had caused no one else any harm. Still, on his deathbed, he confessed to killing the peddler but refused to divulge the place where he had buried him. Local farmers searched for bones but found little save a decayed backpack with trinkets and the old peddler's clothing.

Then in the 1870s, the landowner hired men to dig a new well along the hillside. Upon excavation, workers discovered a decayed corpse beneath some fieldstones. Locals gave the corpse a proper burial, hoping that the ghost would find peace. However, many years later, farmers coming through the area after dark still took a two-mile detour of that lonely spot on the Logan Road to avoid the ghost of the peddler.

Pickaway County

Stages Pond State Nature Preserve
4890 Hagerty Road
Ashville, Ohio 43103
39.671537,-82.936705

The Truth Behind the Dead Screaming Mules

A wagon and team of mules lay at the bottom of Stage's Pond outside Ashville. A story about their haunting the pond area has been passed down from a local family to volunteers and staff at the preserve and verified by a descendant of the farmer.

Sometimes when a good storm rolls over Stages Pond State Nature Preserve, you can hear the deep thud of hooves bolting across muddy roads and then the splash of swampy water as if something huge is bursting headlong into the boggy marsh there. Afterward, feral and terrified screams echo ghostly cries in the air before they vanish as if swallowed up.

More than one visitor to the preserve has been startled by this commotion. But, when they ask locals, they do not always believe the truth told—that on a muggy August day in the 1800s, a farmer who lived across Ward Road was taking in the hay. A storm blew across the fields, and he ran to get out of the rain. Lightning bolted across the sky along with an explosion of thunder right after. The wagon team he was using to take in the hay bolted down over the road and across the muddy land around Stage's Pond. Straight into the marshy, quick-sand-like muck they went, mired and fighting until they sank so deeply no one could retrieve them. Now, only their ghostly echoes fill the thick air on hot summer nights, and right before a storm when lightning fills the sky and thunder rolls nearby.

Union County

Stretch Along Union County and Logan County Line

Bigfoot Takes a Stroll Through the Country

Bigfoot was seen in Logan and Union counties in the 1980s.

In the heat of a 1980 summer, Bigfoot strolled through more than a few farm fields in Logan and Union counties. Credible witnesses included a Russells Point police officer who saw the 400-pound, 7 to 9 foot hairy and neckless beast while unloading pigs on his property. A local game protector and his wife joked about the sightings until she saw it driving along the roadway. Cars lined up to catch a peek at the monster, but it disappeared as quickly as it came.

Franklin County

Schiller Park
1000 City Park Avenue
Columbus, Ohio 43206
39.941830, -82.994666

Has No Head in Columbus

Schiller Park where a ghost appeared.

In mid-November of 1894, a 54-year-old wine agent for Brandt and Company in Toledo named Albert Dittelbach was visiting the city of Columbus for business. Those around him noticed he was somewhat downcast, but no one expected to find him dead in the popular Schiller Park in German Village. He had committed suicide by shooting himself in the head.

Schiller Park in its earlier years and around the time of the ghostly sightings.

Less than two weeks after Dittelbach's death, William Bell and a friend were returning from a party and took a shortcut through the dark, deserted park. Within the park's limits, they noticed a figure draped in a gray robe from shoulders to knees. He was pacing back and forth with hands outstretched along the walkway directly in front of the Schiller Monument. Curious, the two paused to take in the lone stranger, and they saw he had no head.

On a cold, sunny Tuesday in January and well over 120 years later, I walked the old city park in Columbus where Dittelbach ended his life. I stopped at the Schiller Monument, hoping to see anything that resembled a spirit. Maybe it was too light or too cold or the wrong time of year, but I did not see the ghost. I do not give up that easily. I think I will wait for the more haunting time of the year and try again.

Delaware County

Sulphur Spring
50 S Henry Street
Delaware, Ohio 43015
40.296885, -83.065191

Of Ghosts and Hidden Treasures

By using this site of an old relic from a long-gone sanitorium as a mapping guide along with a ghost's guiding hand, steps could be taken toward Bokes Creek, a tributary of the Scioto to find a treasure in the 6-miles somewhere between.

If you are walking just off Henry Street and across the road from Selby Stadium at Ohio Wesleyan University in Delaware, you may not even notice a stone-walled garden area with a large marble bowl tucked on the north side of Phillips Hall. However, in the 1800s, this little area was a focal point for one of Ohio's greatest ghostly treasure hunts.

Bokes Creek—where a treasure hunt ensued and a Delaware
Indian ghost would walk the muddy shores.

It all starts at Bokes Creek, about a 14-minute drive from
the little stone-walled garden area. Bokes Creek is a small
tributary of the Scioto River near the city of Delaware. It
may not seem like much as far as waterways are concerned.
When you drive past it along OH-37, you may only know it
is nearby by the thickness of the brush on either side of its
banks. But along its muddy shores, the ghost of a chief of the
Delaware people would frequently appear in the mid-1800s
between the darkest hours of dusk to dawn. For many years
and at frequent intervals, the spirit would pace back and
forth as if searching desperately for something near the
ground where he had tread. Then just as ephemerally as he
appeared, he would fade away.

After a time, the novelty of the ghost haunting Bokes
Creek wore off. Legends began to spring up again around
this wandering spirit in December of 1894 when he started
to appear again. People remembered the ghost because they
recalled a wild treasure hunt the last time the spirit had
appeared regularly around 1869.

At that time, an old man adopted into the Delaware tribe during his younger years reported his Indian family knew of a silver mine. The location was between the area where the ghost appeared on Bokes Creek and a particular mineral spring in the city of Delaware where, by using a series of steps beginning at the said spring, it would lead toward Bokes Creek and the silver. This mineral spring was a part of the old White Sulphur Springs, a resort from the 1830s. This health sanitorium eventually went out of business before the purchase of land for Ohio Wesleyan. However, because the old man was not born into the tribe, he was never given its exact location.

In that year, treasure hunters descended upon the quiet little town of Delaware and the over 6-mile span of land between Bokes Creek and the tiny mineral spring. They believed the ghost had returned to show the location of the treasure. But for all the hunting and digging, no one recovered the treasure. Walls were eventually put up to protect the spring, and along with the treasure hunters, the stories faded away.

The ghost may still appear along Bokes Creek. The road nearby is not too heavily traveled. Few passersby may even see him pacing along the shores. The mineral spring that became a focal point during the ghostly treasure hunt can still be seen. It is the beautiful, little stone-walled garden area with the marble bowl located near Phillips Hall on the grounds of Ohio Wesleyan University.

Delaware County

Henry Street
S Henry Street
Delaware, Ohio 43015
40.295976, -83.064468

The Red Slipper Murder

Henry Street in Delaware where a ghostly murder victim walks.

A squirrel hunter found the mysterious girl's body clad only in a flannel nightgown and red, one-strap slippers in September of 1953. She was dumped near a deserted roadside along Route 53 in Wyandot County 3 miles north of Upper Sandusky, her face so severely mashed that it was unidentifiable. But local police traced the serial number inside the red slippers from Columbus shoe manufacturer Prima Footwear that distributed their products to a department store in White Plains, New York. Unofficial police reports from White plains showed a young woman, blue-eyed Cynthia Pfeil, had been missing since August 24th. With a photo of Cynthia in hand, police marched to the department store where they sold the slippers.

One clerk recalled selling the shoes to the girl only two days before she disappeared. Shortly after, the police headed to the home of Cynthia's parents, who stated they were unsure of their daughter's whereabouts. However, they believed she was with a boyfriend, Roger Schinagle, whom they did not approve of, but Cynthia met when they attended the university together a year ago.

Slim, clean-cut, and sandy-haired, the 19-year-old Ohio Wesleyan sophomore the police brought in for questioning shortly after hardly fit the profile of a murderer. But they did not know his dark and explosive side. Cynthia had returned home after her freshman year and began work in Cleveland. Roger worked for a trucking company, and when he was not in school, he drove through Cleveland to see her.

Cynthia snuck down to see Roger in Delaware, stating she had to tell him something. He set her up in the equipment shed at the south athletic field on the campus because she could not afford a hotel room. However, Roger would not allow her to leave as he did not want anyone to know she was there. While Cynthia was cooped up, she wandered outside the shed, and a groundskeeper spotted her and told Roger. In a fury, Roger dragged her back, beating and choking her to death. Then, the college student brutally smashed her face with 17 gashes from a lead pipe so she would not be recognizable. He dumped her body in an isolated area 35 miles away from campus.

Roger Schinagle was arrested, found guilty, and went to prison for ten years. Cynthia's family buried the 19-year-old girl in White Plains—she had been two months pregnant, and Roger admitted the child was his own. But her story is far from over. Cynthia walks Henry Street near her murder site. Some have even heard her wailing as she strolls along the route.

Madison County

Red Brick Tavern
1700 Cumberland Road (Route 40)
Lafayette, Ohio 43140
39.938304,-83.406515

Embroidered Sampler Stained Blood Red

Red Brick Tavern

Built around 1836/1837 along the National Road halfway between Columbus and Springfield, it became the second oldest stagecoach stop in Ohio, with 24 rooms for travelers. Six presidents have stopped there on their journeys. In its time, it acted as a private schoolhouse from 1854 to 1864 run by the Minter sisters (there were six of them) who lived there. The Red Brick Tavern has a ghost story to tell: One of the Minter girls became ill and committed suicide. Her spirit roams the second floor. An embroidered sampler she was making states 'Remember Me.' It now sits in the second-floor hallway and is stained blood red due to her ghostly hands.

Morrow County

Vails Cross Roads
Centerburg, Ohio 43011
40.365119,-82.753447
to
Bloomfield Cemetery
40.378901,-82.723449

A Strange Confession

A ghostly rider once roamed this road.

A ghost rides on horseback in Vail's Cross Roads along the area where West Liberty-Mt Vernon Road crosses OH-656. It travels about two miles along OH-656 until the highway forms a sharp veer to the right at Rich Hill Bloomfield Road. There it stops at the Bloomfield Cemetery and vanishes. The ghost's story goes like this:

During the late 1800s, there was a house at Vail's Cross Roads in Morrow County. It was tumbledown and vacant, a home many would reside in, but few would remain for long.

However, it was not always empty. Salo Bintern lived in the house in the 1850s, along with his wife and four sons. The father was frugal and kept to himself. He seemed honest but always gave an impression of having more money than his meager farm would appear to produce. He would appear and then disappear from home for days at a time. There were always suspicious rumors amongst his neighbors questioning his whereabouts, yet no one could pinpoint any mischief he might have caused.

One day a wealthy stock buyer came to town looking for a place to farm. He stopped for a few days at the Vail's Hotel owned by Benjamin and Mary Vail. It was not long before Salo Bintern popped into the inn, too, from his home nearby. He conversed with the traveler, suggesting he might show the man around the community and help him find an attractive piece of property. Old Bintern also invited the prospective land buyer to stay at his home so the two could leave at an early hour the next morning and not awaken the others staying at the inn. The stock buyer agreed and went home with Bintern that evening.

After that, no one ever saw the wealthy stock buyer again. He disappeared. Now, this would be of little significance because people do come and go. There was only one problem—travelers along the route found his horse the following day minus the rider and the saddlebags. Bintern bought a brand new farm. Years would pass, and sometime later, people started seeing the ghost, although they could not identify to whom it belonged. That is, until one day, a strange old man appeared in the infirmary in Morrow County looking for a comfortable place to die. He refused to give his personal information at first, then finding out he must offer up some evidence that he was a resident to receive a room at the institution, the old man divulged his name was Bintern. He was a local in the county long ago.

It was easy to tell that he would not be there long when the dying man settled in. After staying there for about two weeks, he asked permission to meet privately with the infirmary superintendent, and of course, the administrators granted the request. When the superintendent arrived, Bintern told him he had a admission, but he must have the superintendent's solemn word that it would not be shared until he was dead. The superintendent agreed and received a full confession pertaining to a stranger who had visited Vail's Cross Roads years ago.

After, the superintendent secretly went to the house and found within bits of saddlebags where the dying man stated they would be located. Bintern had beaten the stock buyer to death while he slept in the bed at his homestead. But if the killer divulged his misdeed, does that murdered traveler still ride the roadway to the cemetery and stop there? Some say he does.

Vail Cross Roads. Does a ghost still travel these roads? I have not seen him on my trips through—*yet*, that is.

Richland County

Ohio State Reformatory
100 Reformatory Road
Mansfield, Ohio 44905
40.782686,-82.502875

Mansfield Prison Ghosts

Ohio State Reformatory or Mansfield Prison in 1907.

When the Ohio State Reformatory in Mansfield was open, 1896 to 1990, over 154,000 inmates passed through the gates. In addition, the prison took in offenders who were too old for juvenile corrections or who also committed less severe crimes than those sent to prison at the Ohio State Penitentiary in Columbus. The goal of this institution was to reform inmates with education, religion, and learning trades.

The reformatory was not always successful, and not everyone made it out alive. Two hundred people died at the jail, including guards killed in escape attempts. Frank Hanger, a 48-year-old guard, was beaten to death with an iron bar by Chester Probaski and Elza Chandler in October of 1932. He was making rounds in the disciplinary block, and Chandler was crouching near a cupboard. Chandler was on an extended stay in solitary confinement. Prison wardens shuffled both murderers to the electric chair.

Even outside its walls, there was a tragedy. In July of 1948, Robert Daniels and 22-year-old John West, former prisoners, kidnapped and murdered John Niebel, his wife Nolana, and their 21-year-old daughter, Phyllis. John Niebel had been superintendent of the 1600 acre honor farm for 20 years. The men planned the revenge murder for four years.

The family of the warden lived at the reformatory. In November of 1950, the warden's wife, Helen Bauer Glattke, died of pneumonia several days after an accidental discharge of a gun in the superintendent's home inside the prison. While reaching into a closet to retrieve a jewelry box, the gun discharged, injuring the woman. Arthur Lewis Glattke, her husband, died following a heart attack suffered in his office on February 10th, 1959. This is the closet where the gun discharged, injuring Helen, which eventually caused her death. Her ghostly voice is heard quietly chattering in the room and around the closet.

Most of those 200 who died in the Ohio State Reformatory were from diseases like flu and tuberculosis. Others had more violent deaths which occurred around these cell blocks.

The Mansfield Reformatory Preservation Society runs the remaining parts of the building—the original East (and six tiers of the world's largest free-standing steel cell block) and West Cell Blocks and administration section. The building is open for tours. If you go, expect to see, hear, or feel ghosts. We did. My 4-year-old shushed me with forefinger to lips because, as he put it: "Mommy, there's a man trying to sleep in that bed." Not long after, I took a picture of my daughter with a full-body apparition showing up in the image.

A priceless family picture—my daughter digesting that her brother is telling her there is a ghost a foot away. *And* he is not a happy ghost. We woke him up. *Shhhh.*

A ghost walks into the room behind her.

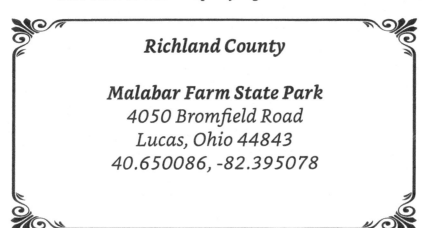

Richland County

Malabar Farm State Park
4050 Bromfield Road
Lucas, Ohio 44843
40.650086, -82.395078

Ghost of Celia Rose

Celia Rose—The sweet face
of a killer—perhaps?

It was a warm June morning in the summer of 1896. David Rose, a local miller who lived in the community of Pleasant Valley, made a mad rush for the nearby doctor in Newville. His wife, Rebecca, had become violently sick two hours after breakfast with vomiting and convulsions. Before David returned to the house with the village doctor, he would also succumb to the same mysterious sickness. It would not be long after that David's 39-year-old son, Walter, was found along the road overcome with the same symptoms.

Six days later, David Rose died an agonizing death. On July 4th, Walter would die. For a short time, Rebecca seemed to be recuperating. She appeared in good health, only to give way to the condition a little less than a month from the day she got sick. She, too, died. The youngest member of the family, a mentally disabled daughter named Celia, fondly called Ceely, was the only one who would not become ill from the symptoms. Autopsies later revealed poisoning with Rough on Rats was what caused the deaths.

Fingers pointed to the childlike Celia Rose. Although she had attended school, she was much farther behind than the other children and spent most of her time alone. At times, Celia found it difficult to differentiate between right and wrong, and her stuttering left her the object of ridicule by bullying children and teens in the community.

To make matters worse, the young Celia, who most thought odd for her disability, was infatuated with a neighbor boy who did not return her fondness, mistaking his kindness for affection. Her innocent trips to visit him had become so frequent, the young man's father had spoken to David Rose, asking him to curtail Celia's visits and affections. Her father, a kind man who was said to scold his daughter rarely, reprimanded her. Some believed this set the circumstances leading to the family's deaths. During her family's illness and after their deaths, she seemed blissfully unaware of the weight of the situation; she probably had no clue what she had done would make them go away forever.

A local prosecutor connived with Theresa Davis, a former classmate of Celia, to trick her into confessing. Theresa pretended to be Celia's friend, who must have been exhilarating for the young woman who had never had a chum before. Theresa told Celia she had kept the secrets of others who had done things to those who had been mean to them, and Celia could confide anything to her.

Celia allegedly confessed she had poisoned her family with arsenic and added it to their morning cottage cheese because her father disapproved of her seeing the boy next door. Twenty-three-year-old Celia Rose was found guilty of the murders. The verdict took only an hour. She was sentenced to life in prison, then acquitted on the grounds of insanity. She was sent to the Lima State Hospital and died there on March 14th, 1934. The little white farmhouse of Celia Rose and her family is at Malabar Farm State Park. It is haunted. Celia's ghostly younger self returns to the home and is said to peer through the windows.

Watch for ghostly Celia peering through the windows when you pass this little farmhouse. Did she poison her family or not? Some say Celia was manipulated into making a confession, and that is why her ghost returns—to right the wrong of those who coerced this young woman to lie for the real killer because she had no one left in the world to defend her.

Marion County

Old City Hall and Fire Department
*Corner of S Prospect and
W Church Streets
Marion, Ohio 43302
40.587435,-83.13004*

Ghost of the One-Legged Shoestring Peddler

City Hall in the early 1900s where one-legged, dead Shoestring Jack could be heard dragging his leg across the floor.

In 1909, prisoners confined at the Marion Jail often complained of seeing the ghost of a one-legged shoestring peddler, nicknamed 'Shoestring Jack,' who had committed suicide in Cell 1 only six months earlier. He had hung himself to death by tying a pair of his shoestrings about his neck and choking himself to death.

The sleeping quarters for the city firemen who were on duty were located just above the jail. Ira Shrock, a local fireman, reported that he was awakened at night more than once by the crunch and grind of the dead shoestring peddler's wooden leg dragging across the gritty cement floor. *Crunch. Drag. Crunch. Drag. Crunch.* Not far behind came the ghostly apparition of the shoestring peddler himself. Ira Shrock did not sleep well.

Where the city hall and fire department once stood is a parking lot. Perhaps the ghost still wanders there!

The Old City Hall and Fire Department building was on the corner of South Prospect and W Church Streets in Marion. It is not there anymore. Instead, a parking lot has taken its place. I wonder if folks parking there at night still hear the crunch and drag of that old peg leg of Shoestring Jack's working its way across the cement floor—*Crunch. Drag. Crunch. Drag. Crunch..* Or perhaps if you have parked there before, now that you know about the ghost of the one-legged shoestring peddler, you will not use the lot there anymore.

Knox County

Camp Sychar
201 Sychar Road
Mt Vernon, Ohio 43050
40.406204, -82.469265

Ghostly Guardian of the Spring

Camp Sychar—in its early years. It had a ghost. Probably still does. *Courtesy: The Denzer Collection Knox Times.*

In the 19th century, a holiness movement began, and religious camp meetings were held across the U.S. by various churches, including the Methodist Church. The Ohio State Camp Meeting Association held camp meetings in multiple cities until transporting the tents from town to town became a hardship. Undeterred, they settled on a rural area about 2 miles outside the city proper of Mt. Vernon and built a campground and accommodations for people to stay during the meetings.

Because of the fresh spring that came from within the camp, they named it Camp Sychar for a deep well in the Bible, denoted by 'Well of Sychar.' The pure spring water was so good at this new camp outside Mt. Vernon that they wanted to share it with the community. A pipe was laid to a trough about 50 feet away and along the main roadside outside this little camping village. People would come from miles around to drink the fresh, cold water from Camp Sychar.

Not long after dedicating the camp, strange stories began popping up about a peculiar apparition seen moving about the spring. The ghostly figure would pace noiselessly back and forth by the spring, then vanish. Two theories revolved around the spirit—a hermit once lived near the spring, and perhaps it was his ghost returning to guard the waters or an old Bible-toting minister who was particularly fond of preaching near the spring.

Camp Sychar well—Perhaps when passing, you will see the spirit, whether minister or hermit, still guarding its beloved spring.

Licking County

The Licking County Historic Jail
46 S 3rd Street
Newark, Ohio 43055
40.056171, -82.401398

Ghosts of Serial Killers, Murderers, Insane, and a Sweet Kid from Kentucky Lynched by a Ruthless Mob

Carl Etherington — teen lynched by a rabid mob.

The Licking County Jail. The front three levels housed the sheriff's family and a jail matron. The rear held 32 jail cells, each 8' x 8' in size. —*Image: Library of Congress*

Built in 1889, the Licking County Jail has housed serial killers, murderers, and the insane. On January 6th, 1947, Missus Laura Belle Devlin, dubbed the Handsaw Slayer stayed there. She murdered and then dismembered her 72-year-old husband's corpse with a sickle and saw, then tossed the remains into their coal stove to dispose of the evidence.

There were at least 22 deaths within those walls, seven of those being suicides. Four of the deaths were sheriffs who died from heart attacks. And there was one informal lynching—

Conservative religious factions had revived the Prohibition Movement in the early 1900s. By 1910, it was in full swing as were more than 80 saloons and 30 brothels in the city of Newark. The Ohio Anti-Saloon League was a lobbying organization whose crusade was to stop the consumption and sale of alcohol. In the summer of 1910, they decided to flex their muscles and show their strength. The group set their sights on Newark and were dead-set on putting a stop to the scandalous selling of alcohol, along with prostitution and gambling right along the city streets. They were not only tired of the local police's inability to stop the illicit behavior, but also turning a blind eye to liquor violations. They knew Sheriff William Linke was taking protection money from bars which he would not close.

League President Wayne Wheeler hired a few private detectives from Cleveland and had them deputized before the upcoming raid at 8:30 a.m. July 8th. Next, the men set out to sweep several local saloons and arrest the owners. The raids did not fare well. One group of marshals was trapped in a bar by a mob of angry drunks and had to flee out the back door. One marshal, 17-year-old Carl Etherington red-headed and hailing from Kentucky, made a desperate run from the ruffians, jumping on to the interurban streetcar.

He was able to ride for a couple of miles only to be stopped by 41-year-old William Howard. An ex-Newark cop, Howard was now proprietor of the Last Chance Saloon. He began beating Etherington with a blackjack until the teen fell to the blows. But as Etherington went to the ground, he drew his revolver and shot Howard in the stomach.

Almost instantly, a crowd came upon Etherington and beat him severely, then dragged him to a cell at the Licking County Jail. When word came that evening that Howard had died, at 10:30 p.m., a mob tore up the railroad tracks for a tie and violently bashed the cell door in. Even as the horrified teen listened to the sound of the door crashing outside, he was more concerned about his mother as he sobbed to the guard: "What will mother say when she hears of this?"

Etherington was hanged on July 8th, 1910 from this pole on the southeast corner of the courthouse square—intersection at the corner of South Park Place and 2nd Streets.
39 S Park Place Newark, Ohio 43055 (40.057460, -82.400626)
Image: Newark Advocate and Licking County Historical Society

They proceeded to beat him again savagely and some say until he died in that cell. But it was not enough. They whisked the teen outside and hanged him from a telegraph pole while thousands, including children, watched. The macabre lynching would end in 20 to 25 first-degree murder indictments, removal of the county sheriff, and the resignation of the mayor.

It also may have left behind ghosts from its violent past. Doors slam. Cries of help ring out, and footsteps pad along the floors. Shadowy figures walk the hallways, and there is an occasional jingle of keys. But why not find out about its ghostly past yourself? You might run into poor Carl Etherington or part of his crazed lynching mob, or even the Handsaw Slayer, herself. The Licking County Governmental Preservation Society oversees the Licking County Historic Jail. They offer both historical and paranormal tours.

Citations

Johnny's Grave:
—Johnny N. Morehouse. (n.d.). Retrieved from https://
www.findagrave.com/memorial/731/johnny-n_-morehouse
Scotts Creek:
—Awful Calamity - A Young Man and His Wife Drowned in Scotts Creek.
(n.d.). The Hocking Sentinel Logan, Ohio 18 Aug 1887
Moonville Tunnel:
—Quackenbush, J. (2017). Moonville. Its Past. Its Ghosts. Its Legends. 21
Crows Dusk to Dawn Publishing
—The Fort Wayne Weekly November 10th 1880
—Athens Messenger, Thursday, Nov 11, 1880
—February 1895 Chillicothe Gazette
Lincoln Ghost Train:
—Ghost-Hunting Groups Enjoy Renewed Popularity. Hannah, James.
Associated Press.
Darby-Lee Cemetery:
Ohio Ghost Hunter Guide VIII –Jannette Quackenbush
Stumpy's Hollow:
—The Ohio Guide By Federal Writers' Project, Writers' Program (Ohio)
—The Times Recorder, Zanesville, Ohio Thursday 2 October 1947
—The_Zanesville Signal March 1, 1946
Elmore Rider:
—The News Messenger Fremont June 11,1927
—Cleveland Plain Dealer November 24, 1922
—The News Messenger Fremont Sep 21, 1942
Lucy Run:
—Historical Collections of Ohio An Encyclopedia of the State: History
Both General and Local, Geography ... Sketches of Eminent and
Interesting Characters, Etc., Vol 1, Henry Howe H. Howe & Son, 1889
—Ancestry.com: Ezekiel Dimmit family tree, Charles Robinson family
Dimmit, 1830, 1940, 1860 census.
—Springfield Globe Republic, November 29, 1885
—rootsweb.ancestry.com/~ohclecgs/cemeteries/lucyrun/index.html
—Hilda Lindner Knapp. Batavia Branch Reference Librarian, Clermont Co
—www.findagrave.com/cgi-bin/fg.cgi?
page=gr&GSfn=lucy&GSiman=1&GScid=41885&GRid=21564866&
Fallsville:
—Penn Township, Careytown, Dodsonville, Samantha, Russel, Boston
Fairview: Highland County 1916H
—Highland County Map: 1887
—Rootsweb.com
—Findagrave.com
—Buckeye Legends: Folktales and lore from Ohio By Michael Jay Katz
Willoughby's Mysterious Girl in Blue:
—U.S. Census 1920
—Evening Independent-Apr 19,1934-p-10 "Girl in Blue Still a Mystery"
—Sandusky Register-5/13/1936-p-12 "May Solve Mystery of Girl in Blue"
—Sandusky Register-July 4, 1936 page1 "Girl in Blue Identified"
Louisa Catherine Fox:
—Coshocton Age September 24, 1869 -Almost A Suicide
—The Herald And Torch Light (Hagerstown, Md) February 17, 1869—A
Terrible Tragedy in Ohio
—New Philadelphia Ohio Democrat 2/12/1869— Young Girl's Throat Cut
By Her Lover—The Murderer Attempts Suicide
—Hagerstown Mail Hagerstown Maryland February 5, 1869
—Greencastle Weekly Indiana Press March 30, 1870—The Scaffold
Salem Methodist Episcopal Cemetery:
—Centennial History of Belmont County, Ohio, and RepCitizens, A. T.
McKelvey, Biographical Publishing Company, 1903 - Belmont County OH
Old Man's Cave:
—The Hocking Sentinel. June 22, 1905. The Wonderland of Hocking

Dead Man's Cave
—Logan Hocking Sentinel July 21, 1853
—The Democrat-sentinel., August 12, 1909
—The Democrat-sentinel., August 15, 1907
—The Democrat-sentinel., February 25, 1909
—The Democrat-sentinel., March 28, 1907
—The Hocking sentinel., June 22, 1905, Image 4 old man hid money
Mary Stockum:
—Ancestry.com—Stockum
—www.sleepyhollowpumpkins.com/legend_marystockum.htm
—www.graveaddiction.com/stockum.html
—1870 US Census—Linton Twp, Coshocton County
—Profile by Joanna Ross. (1967, Nov 11) Coshocton Tribune
-Map: Linton Township, Bacon P.O., Maysville, Plainfield P.O., Jacobsport
Atlas: Coshocton County 1872
Mary Seneff Ghost:
—York Township, Mechanicsburg—Atlas: Tuscarawas County 1875
—The Stark County Democrat., March 03, 1881, Image
—Cleveland Plain Dealer. Ohio News 1881-03-16
—The Eaton Democrat., Mary Seneffs Ghost. April 07, 1881
—The Eaton Democrat. Ohio State News. April 14, 1881
—Memphis daily appeal. The Ghost of Murdered Woman Visits the
Glimpses of the Moon. March 18, 1881.
—The Stark County Democrat. Missus Ellen A. Athey. March 03, 1881
—The Ohio Democrat. Murder Most Foul. New Phila Ohio, June 17, 1880
—The Ohio Democrat. The Murder of Mary Seneff. July 8, 1880
—The Ohio Democrat. The Murder of Miss Mary Seneff. June 24, 1880.
Turzillo, Jane A. Wicked Women of Northeast Ohio. The History Press,
2011
Lick Road:
—https://creepycincinnati.com/2019/10/13/lick-road-and-the-legend-
of-amy/
—http://www.weirdus.com/states/ohio/road_less_traveled/lick_road/
index.php
Lucas County:
—Weber, Lauren. Toledo Blade. http://www.toledoblade.com/
frontpage/2007/06/17/Beneath-the-beams-abutments-and-concrete-
Toledo-s-Maumee-crossings-have-a-story-to-tell.html
—Cincinnati Enquirer Dec 28, 1884. A Ghost on the Bridge
Johnson's Island:
—New York Times. August 13, 2000. Archipelago of Legends.
Mustapha Island:
—The Pittsburgh Press Aug 8,1939
Cherry Fork Cemetery:
—Cleveland Plain Dealer, Historical Archives August 12, 1896 A Grave
Yawns.
—The News-Herald. Hillsboro, Oh. January 18, 1894. Couldn't Get His
Breath
—News-Herald. Hillsboro, Oh. Thursday December 27, 1893 Parker
Confesses
—The Evening World. New York, NY. January 12, 1894, BROOKLYN LAST
EDITION, HANGED BY BEST CITIZENS. Boy Murderer Victim of Mob Law
in Ohio
—The News-Herald. Hillsboro, Oh. December 28, 1893, Page 5. An Awful
Double Crime
—The Evening Bulletin. Maysville, KY. December 27, 1893.
Woman in Black:
—SPECIAL DISPATCH TO THE ENQUIRER. Cincinnati Enquirer July 17,
1888. WOMAN AND CHILD.
Old City Hall and Fire Department:
—Marion Weekly Star-4/2/09 Ghost Limps —Through Cells and Corridors

Bloody Bridge:
—The Bloody Bridge- Old Papers Recall Bloody Tragedy in the Palmy Days of the Canal. May 15th, 1908 Delphos Daily Herald Newspaper
Celia Rose:
—Celia Rose—www.findagrave.com/cgi-bin/fg.cgi?page=cr&CRid=43582
—Ironwood News Record September 19, 1896
—Daily Iowa Capital August 14, 1896
—Decatur Evening Bulletin August 14, 1896
—Galveston Daily News August 14, 1896
—Newark Daily Advocate October 21, 1896
—Portsmouth Daily Times October 14, 1896
—Reno Weekly Gazette And Stockman August 20, 1896
—Triple Murder: The Crimes Committed by Celia Rose By Brett Mitchell
Ashtabula Train Disaster:
—Escher, S.(2009,). I-35 Bridge Collapse: Ashtabula River Railroad Disaster .
—Ashtabula River Railroad Disaster . 35wbridge.pbworks.com/w/page/900664/Ashtabula%20River%20Railroad%20Disaster
—The Milan exchange., January 11, 1877, Image 2
—The Tiffin tribune., January 04, 1877, Image 3
—National Republican., Washington DC, 12/ 30, 1876, Horror of Horrors
—Wilson, H.(1884, July 2). A Prize Venture. Abbeville Press and Banner,
River Styx Bridge Train Wreck:
—ENGINEER KILLED And Fireman Fatally Injured by a Wreck on the Erie. Mansfield News, Mansfield, OH 22 Mar 1899
—Rittman, OH Train Wreck, Mar 1899. NEEDS LAUNDERING. Badly Damaged Mail Brought in From the Wreck at Rittman. Mansfield News, Mansfield, OH 23 Mar 1899
—Milton Township Atlas: Wayne County 1897
Buckland Lock/Lock 44:
—Akron Daily Democrat. July 21, 1902, Page 5. A Weird Tale of the Canal Locks Near Napoleon
Beaver Creek State Park:
—Ira F. Mansfield; Robin Hood Club. Little Beaver River valleys, Penns— Ohio with illustrated check list of flowers and essays. 1914
—The Legend of Gretchen's Lock. (n.d.). Retrieved from https://www.carnegie.lib.oh.us/gretchen
Dead Man Hollow:
—Portsmouth Times May 31, 1948 . Grave In the 'Wilds' Of Scioto Co Holds Secret
—Harry Knighton, "Shawnee Forest," undated typescript, Digital History Lab Collection, Clark Memorial Library, Shawnee SU, Portsmouth, Ohio.
Bailey Bridge:
—http://cuyahogafallshistory.com/2013/03/murder-by-the-doodlebug/
—Holland, Jeri. Historian. Cuyahoga Falls Historical Society 2015. based off a written interview with Gilbert Roberts, local history and court transcripts. Cuyahoga Falls Historical Society 2015 http://cuyahogafallshistory.com/2014/10/the-headless-ghost-on-bailey-road/
—The Ohio star., Ravenna, Ohio. April 20, 1853 Supposed Murder of a Stranger-Evidences of Foul Play
—Wheeling daily intelligencer., April 26, 1853. Horrid Murder.
—True American., June 13, 1855 Steubenville, Ohio Execution of Parks
—The Ohio star., January 18, 1854. Parks Sentenced
—The Belmont Chronicle, and Farmers, Mechanics and Manufacturers advocate., January 27, 1854. Conviction and Sentence of Parks.
—The Bench and Bar of Cleveland. Page 96
—The Last Days of Cleveland: And More True Tales of Crime and Disaster from By John Stark Bellamy
Haunted Tunnel:
—http://seekinglostsouls.com/category/ohiohauntings/page/4/

—https://www.youtube.com/watch?v=AFVIpgpIkk4, Ashland Tunnel, Twp rd 1536. Brd Pritt. Nov 15, 2009
Dead Man's Hollow:
-Murder. Huron Reflector (October 25, 1836)
—History of Crawford County, Ohio and representative citizens, John E. Hopley,Published 1912 by Richmond-Arnold Pub. Co. in Chicago, Ill. (pg 547 - 548) Dead Man's Hollow
Seneca:
—Daughters of the American Revolution. Ohio Society. Dolly Todd Madison Chapter. (1915). Ohio Early State and Local History.
—Lisa Swickard/Virgin Alley Press.Retrieved from https:// www.hauntedtiffin.com/sites-cqnr
Ohio Wesleyan:
—HIS SPIRIT: VISITS THE THREE HILLS, SAID TO CONTAIN UNTOLD RICHES IN SPECIAL DISPATCH TO THE ENQUIRER Cincinnati Enquirer (1872-1922); Dec 21, 1894.
Milan Cemetery:
—Haunted History. (n.d.). Retrieved from www.facebook.com/ historyhaunted/posts/history-haunting-of-milan-cemetery-broad-street -milan-ohio-usamilanis-a-village-/1345819378777472/
Goll Woods:
—genealogy.com/forum/regional/states/topics/oh/fulton/193/
Deep Cut:
—31 Oct 1991, 8 - The Times Recorder Deep Cut Ghost
Anna Belle:
—Findagrave.com
—Hardin County: By Ronald I. Marvin Jr.
Camp Sychar:
—Cincinnati Enquirer, Special Dispatch to the Enquirer. 11/ 21, 1897 Strange Apparition of a Man That Guards the Spring at Camp Sychar
Licking County Jail:
—Centennial of temperance bloodshed unheralded. (n.d.). Retrieved from https://dispatch.com/article/20100414/news/304149670
—Deputy Marshal Carl Mayes Etherington. (n.d.). Retrieved from https:// www.odmp.org/officer/23113-deputy-marshal-carl-mayes-etherington
—The Newark Advocate Newark, Ohio Wednesday, April 13, 2011 Page 1.
—Story Map Journal. (n.d.). Retrieved from arcgis.com/apps/MapJournal/ index.html?appid=3a1545c98143498296f3e5063dff5ad9
Hatchet Man:
—September, 1839—Washington Globe Nov. 28, 1840
—Washington Globe April 26, 1843
Red Brick Tavern:
—Red Brick Tavern: files.usgwarchives.net/pa/berks/history/family/ tall0003.txt historicredbricktavern.com/
Spencerville Cemetery:
—Elyria Chronicle Telegram. July 27, 1989
Fort Piqua Hotel:
—Dayton Daily News Dayton, Ohio Thursday, October 29, 1998 - Pg163
Vails Crossroads:
—The Marion Daily Star (Marion, Ohio)- January 20 1894—A Grewsome Tale. A Morrow County Murder with Ghostly Attachments.
Johnson's Island:
—-Andra-Hogeland, Brandy. Toledo Haunted Places Examiner. Soldiers may still reside on the Johnsons Island Cemetery.www.examiner.com/ article/soldiers-may-still-reside-on-the-johnsons-island-cemetery
—Johnson's Island Preservation Society. www.johnsonsisland.org
—Donmoyer, Ryan J. New York Times. Archipelago of Legends and Play August 13, 2000 pg. TR10
Pike Lake Haunted Stump:
—Darby, Erasmus Foster. The Haunted Stump
—http://artsandsciences.sc.edu/appalachianenglish/node/546

Minerva Gold:
—The Akron Beacon Journal. Akron, Ohio Sunday, June 14, 1953 - Page 86 Minerva's Buried Treasure. (n.d.).
—Legend of the Lost French Gold - Carroll County Convention & Visitors Bureau. (n.d.). Retrieved from https://www.carrollcountyohio.com/ historical/carroll-county-history/legend-of-the-lost-french-gold
Witch's Grave:
—(n.d.). The Akron Beacon Journal Akron, Ohio Monday, July 29, 1963 - Page 42. Mike Patton--Portage's Lost Cemetery Surrounded by Mystery.
—Dealing With The Dead: Mortality and Community in Medieval and Early Modern Europe. (2018). Leiden, Netherlands: BRILL.
—Mulford B. Elliott. (n.d.). Retrieved from https://www.findagrave.com/ memorial/35688660/mulford-b_-elliott
—"Remember Me As You Pass By". (n.d.). Retrieved from https:// www.vastpublicindifference.com/2010/02/remember-me-as-you-pass-by.html
—THE INFAMOUS WITCH'S GRAVEYARD. (n.d.). Retrieved from https:// www.flickr.com/photos/129609706@N02/39996617045
Chester Bedell:
—Chester Bedell. (n.d.). Retrieved from https://www.findagrave.com/ memorial/104280973/chester-bedell
—Ernie Pyle. The Pittsburgh Press Jul 21, 1938 Snakes in Grave Story Just Myth.
—On, B. B. (1940). Ohio: The Ohio Guide. Best Books on (The Cemetery at North Benton).
Lanterman's Mill:
—http://mvps.synthasite.com/lantermans-mill.php
—https://www.youtube.com/watch?v=y7kENE1w1_g
Ghost Hollow-Rootstown:
—https://myspace.com/neohioparanormalteam/mixes/classic-ghost-hollow-in-rootstown-oh-594667
—McGregor, K. (2000). Randolph, Atwater and Rootstown Revisited: Includes New Milford and St. Joseph.
Lock 4:
—Dayton Daily News. 8/17/1969 Old Ohio-Erie Canal Awaits Visitors
Punderson Manor:
—Geauga County's Ghostly Past Revealed in Chilling Tours. (2013, October 17). Retrieved from https://www.geaugamapleleaf.com/ community/geauga-countys-ghostly-past-revealed-in-chilling-tours/
—Sometimes spirits awaken guests at Punderson lodge in Newbury. (2012, October 25). Retrieved from https://www.cleveland.com/west-geauga/2012/10/sometimes_spirits_awaken_guest.html
Salem Reformed Cemetery:
—Baker, J. (n.d.). Local history: Spooky tales surround the headless angel of Saltillo. Retrieved from timesreporter.com/news/20171030/local-history-spooky-tales-surround-headless-angel-of-saltillo
—Meet the Holmes County ghosts Angel of death at Salem Cemetery, old man who lives in a hotel an. (n.d.). Retrieved from https://www.the-daily-record.com/article/20071028/LIFESTYLE/310289498
Tappan Lake:
—https://www.geocaching.com/geocache/GC67H2X_ghostly-tappan?guid=da596fef-21f5-4658-8dc5-6ea6844c7f7e
Bigfoot in Union County:
—http://www.bigfootencounters.com/articles/unioncounty.htm
—https://www.bfro.net/GDB/show_article.asp?id=320
Blue Bridge:
—Charles Parker's War of 1812 Blockhouse: The Historical Record and the Terry Speer Collection of Historic Artifacts. (n.d.). Retrieved from https:// www.academia.edu/41001242/ Charles_Parkers_War_of_1812_Blockhouse_The_Historical_Record_and_ the_Terry_Speer_Collection_of_Historic_Artifacts

—The Haunting at Bluebridge - Researching one of the Firelands' Ghosts. (n.d.). Retrieved from https://goth.net/forums/viewtopic.php?t=1666
—History of the Fire lands, comprising Huron and Erie Counties, Ohio, with illustrations and biographical sketches of some of the prominent men and pioneers : Williams, W. W. (William W.) : Free Download, Borrow, and Streaming : Internet Archive Page 254. (n.d.). Retrieved from https://archive.org/details/historyoffirelan00will/page/n323/mode/2up/search/seymour

Old Paulding County Jail:
—www.newspapers.com/clip/34183276/nancy-eagleson-murdered/
—https://www.toledo.com/events/just-for-fun/2019/05/25/ghost-hunt-old-paulding-county-jail/

Mercer County:
—karenmillerbennett.com/mercer-county/haunted-mercer-county/
—https://www.dailystandard.com/archive/2010-10-30/stories/13331/local-haunts-to-visit---if-you-dare
—http://files.usgwarchives.net/oh/vanwert/churches/Mendon.txt
—https://www.findagrave.com/cemetery/43755/memorial-search?firstName=&lastName=smith&page=1#sr-23333541

Shelby County:
—Staff interviews at Shelby County Historical Society
—https://www.shelbycountyhistory.org/schs/archives/downtownandbuildings/historsiddtna.htm
—https://www.geocaching.com/geocache/GCYRHZ_cry-baby-bridge?guid=6515bf95-47a4-4d06-a89f-b7c225ab4ca7

Fletcher Cemetery:
—https://www.roadsideamerica.com/tip/59457 Clifton Gorge:
—Fields, Jan. Stories Keep Ghosts Alive in Ohio State Parks. Marion Star. October 23, 1987

County Line Ghost:
—https://www.ohioexploration.com/paranormal/hauntings/vanwertcounty/

Van Wert—Woodland:
—A Minister Frightened by a Ghost. Cincinnati Enquirer. July 10, 1887

Monroe Lake:
—https://www.ohioexploration.com/paranormal/hauntings/monroecounty/

Red Slippers:
—Marion Star September 23, 1953 Ohio Wesleyan Student Confesses Slaying of His College Sweetheart Coshocton Tribune. September 23, 1953
—Shaun R. Illingworth. (n.d.). Gardner, Lloyd Part 2. Retrieved from https://oralhistory.rutgers.edu/64-text-html/1692-gardner-lloyd-part-2